EDUCATION IN THE BAHÁ'Í FAMILY

By the same author

PRAYER : A BAHÁ'Í APPROACH (with William Hellaby)

DEATH THE MESSENGER OF JOY (London, Bahá'í Publishing Trust)

Education
in the Bahá'í Family

by

MADELINE HELLABY

GEORGE RONALD
OXFORD

GEORGE RONALD, Publisher
46 High Street, Kidlington, Oxford, OX5 2DN
© MADELINE HELLABY 1987
All Rights Reserved

Hellaby, Madeline
Education in the Bahá'í family.
1. Bahai education of children
I. Title
297'.89'07   BP370

ISBN 0–85398–267–8
ISBN 0–85398–268–6 Pbk

Typeset by Photoprint, Torquay
Printed in England by Billing & Sons Ltd., Worcester

Contents

	To the Reader	ix
1	Education in General	1
	Our goal	1
	An authority higher than ourselves	2
	Fundamental requirements	4
	A basis for infinite progress	5
	The aim of an educator	7
	Three kinds of education	8
	A word of warning	9
2	The Education of Children	11
	A sacred duty	11
	The education of girls	13
	Complementary responsibilities	15
	Children must exert themselves	17
3	Character Training	19
	A hard task	19
	Three kinds of character	21
	The teacher as doctor	22
	Love for God and for His Manifestation	23
	The fear of God	24
	Basic spiritual laws	26

  Truthfulness and trustworthiness 26
  Justice 41 *Moderation* 44 *Self-defence* 45
  Obedience 47 *Courtesy* 53 *Kindness* 55
  Self-discipline 56

	Parents stand as God	57
	Rear children to be staunch in faith	59
	Hardship	60
4	**Family Life**	65
	The mother's rôle	65
	Prayer	73
	Discipline	75
	Family rights	76
	The crossroads	77
	Correction of faults	78
	Appreciation of differences	80
	Difficult children	83
	Consultation	87
	Law and order	90
	Maturity at fifteen	93
	The one-Bahá'í-parent family	97
	Happiness	100
	A positive attitude to life	102
5	**First Teach Your Own Self**	104
	Set the example	104
	Love humanity	105
	Implications	106
	'It matters' and 'I care'	107
	How much does it mean to us?	108
	Standards of decency, dignity and reverence	111
6	**Feasts and Holy Days**	115
	The centre of our worship	115
	Isolated believers	119
	The Nineteen Day Feast 121	
	Holy Days 124	
	Christmas	127
	Intercalary Days	130

7	Tests	133
	God and suffering	133
	The pull of the outside world	136
	A spiritual Everest	143
	We must do the best we can	145
	Conclusion	147
	Epilogue	149
	Appendix	150
	Key to References	155
	References	158

*Dedicated to the memory of
Abu'l-Qásim Faizí
Hand of the Cause of God,
a much loved and respected friend
who first suggested
that I should study education*

To the Reader

This book is not intended to be a manual on child psychology. From that point of view there are as many ways of bringing up children as there are Bahá'í families; but the basic principles are the same for all of us. Most of it is written out of personal experience and I am fully aware that, because of this diversity of approach, others would handle it differently. Indeed, some have already done so; but variety is one of the joys of the Bahá'í Faith, for as Bahá'u'lláh says, 'Know assuredly that just as thou firmly believest that the Word of God, exalted be His glory, endureth for ever, thou must, likewise, believe with undoubting faith that its meaning can never be exhausted.'[1] Each person's insight is but one of the colours of the rainbow that go to make up light.

Because most of what follows was originally delivered as talks, although expanded with additional material, I decided to leave its rather informal style as it stood: I didn't want to edit it so heavily that it became an essay. Only what can be said rather than read has been removed!

The following quotation shows just how much importance is given in the Bahá'í Faith to the education of children, both by 'Abdu'l-Bahá, Who wrote it, and previously, by Bahá'u'lláh Himself, in the *Kitáb-i-Aqdas*, the Most Holy Book:

... in this Cycle, education and training are recorded in the Book of God as obligatory and not voluntary. That is, it is enjoined upon the father and mother, as a duty, to strive with all effort to train the daughter and the son, to nurse them from the breast of knowledge, and to rear them in the bosom of sciences and arts. Should they neglect this matter, they shall be held responsible and worthy of reproach in the presence of the stern Lord.²

It is my earnest hope that Bahá'í parents and others who have the spiritual and material welfare of children at heart, will find in the following pages the guidance and inspiration they seek from the profound and all-embracing Writings of Bahá'u'lláh, 'Abdu'l-Bahá and Shoghi Effendi on this vitally important subject.

Madeline Hellaby
October 1987

These *children are neither Oriental nor Occidental, neither Asiatic nor American, neither European nor African; but they are of the Kingdom*; their native home is heaven and their resort is the Kingdom of 'Abhá.

'Abdu'l-Bahá

. . . *My home is the home of peace. My home is the home of joy and delight. My home is the home of laughter and exaltation. Whoever enters through the portals of this home, must go out with gladsome heart. This is the home of light; whosoever enters here must become illumined. This is the home of knowledge; the one who enters it must receive knowledge. This is the home of love; those who come in must learn the lessons of love; thus may they know how to love each other . . .*

'Abdu'l-Bahá

1

Education in General

Our goal

It is interesting to note how many of the more liberal poets and hymn-writers of the nineteenth century had a vision of the future which is in line with the Bahá'í teachings. Perhaps this is not surprising when one remembers that they were alive during most of the period of Bahá'u'lláh's Revelation and so no doubt came, however unwittingly, under its influence. John Greenleaf Whittier, James Russell Lowell, J. Addington Symonds and others wrote a number of such hymns, including 'O brother man', 'Once to every man and nation' and 'These things shall be'. But whereas these visions were rather vague, however inspiring, we as Bahá'ís are engaged in establishing something quite concrete; and whereas the idea of the Kingdom of God on earth remains for most people an idea which gives them warm feelings but not much more, for us it represents the goal – the quite specific goal – towards which we are working. It is a definite goal which we know will be achieved and which is synonymous with the World Order of Bahá'u'lláh.

However, as Esslemont says, you cannot create a golden society out of leaden individuals.[1] You can only change society in so far as you can change individuals; and you can only change individuals in so far as you can change yourself. As regards telling other people how they should behave, Shoghi Effendi says: 'Each one of us is responsible for one life only, and that is our own.'² It will take us all our time to attend to our own faults and improve our own characters. We have no time to concern ourselves with those of other people. The one exception to this is, of course, our own children. As parents, this is very much our concern.

We must always bear in mind Shoghi Effendi's reported statements: 'The object of life to a Bahá'í is to promote the oneness of mankind' and 'Our aim is to produce a world civilisation which in turn will react on the character of the individual'.³ The family is the basic unit of society. It should be our purpose to produce first in little what we hope ultimately to produce in the world. We must begin with ourselves and work outwards from there.

An authority higher than ourselves

One of the difficulties facing new Bahá'ís who have children is that they cannot work in such an orderly fashion. They have to educate themselves at the same time and this can present a formidable challenge. Not only is there a great deal to learn about the Faith and many books to read, but 'Every other word of Bahá'u'lláh's and 'Abdu'l-Bahá's Writings is a preachment on moral and ethical conduct'.⁴ Sometimes they may feel overwhelmed just because there *is* so much. (This is not to say that those who have been Bahá'ís for some time, or have been brought up in the Faith, do not also feel the need for guidance, but the problem is nothing like so acute for them as it is for new Bahá'ís with families. They will surely have read all the Scriptures and writings of Shoghi Effendi available to us, a number of other books dealing with various aspects of the Faith, and become accustomed to the observances of Bahá'í life before they get married and start having children.) The twice-daily reading requirement ensures that these brave new Bahá'í parents begin to read the Scriptures in a systematic fashion and so deepen themselves gradually, which is the best way to deepen, over the months and years. It should not be a matter for discouragement or feeling paralysed; quite the opposite! It is exciting to think that there is such a wealth of spiritual food in existence to help with every aspect of life – and particularly with the upbringing of their children. Deepening is a life-long process. As Colby Ives said in another connection, 'The thing to do is to get started.'[5]

On the other hand, our safeguard is that *all* members of the family, parents as well as children, look to something higher than themselves: a Revelation to the demands of which we are all subject, no matter what our age. 'Abdu'l-Bahá says:

> All humankind are as children in a school, and the Dawning-Points of Light, the Sources of divine revelation, are the teachers, wondrous and without peer. In the school of realities they educate these sons and daughters, according to teachings from God, and foster them in the bosom of grace, so that they may develop along every line, show forth the excellent gifts and blessings of the Lord, and combine human perfections; that they may advance in all aspects of human endeavour, whether outward or inward, hidden or visible, material or spiritual, until they make of this mortal world a wide-spread mirror, to reflect that other world which dieth not.[6]

If we as parents always remember this, then we are less likely to take the line that parents are as God Almighty and shall not be asked of their doings. There is no age limit for the moral law, no double standard of behaviour. Bahá'u'lláh does not give one code of morals for children and another for grown-ups. He makes no distinction as to age.

His standards apply to everyone, young and old alike: if we wouldn't do it or say it in front of the children, then we shouldn't do it or say it at all. By this is meant, for instance, such things as the use of bad language, or telling our child to say to an unwelcome visitor that we aren't in – which is not only untrue in itself but is also teaching the child to be dishonest.

Fundamental requirements

The all-important subject of education can be thought of as training in the fundamental requirements given by 'Abdu'l-Bahá in *Tablets of the Divine Plan*: firmness in the Covenant, love and fellowship, and teaching. Firmness in the Covenant means recognition of the Manifestation of God and obedience to His commands, a spiritual and individual matter first and foremost; love and fellowship means putting our faith into practice, a practical and social matter; and teaching can be seen as a measure of our faith.

We have decreed, O people, that the highest and last end of all learning be the recognition of Him Who is the Object of all knowledge.[7]

The source of all learning is the knowledge of God, exalted be His Glory, and this cannot be attained save through the knowledge of His Divine Manifestation.[8]

The beginning of all things is the knowledge of God, and the end of all things is strict observance of whatsoever hath been sent down from the empyrean* of the Divine Will that pervadeth all that is in the heavens and all that is on the earth.[9]

Say: Teach ye the Cause of God, O people of Bahá, for God hath prescribed unto every one the duty of proclaiming His

---

* *Empyrean*: the highest heaven, where the pure element of fire was supposed to subsist; the heavens.
Empyreal: formed of pure fire or light; pertaining to the highest and purest region of heaven; sublime. (*Chambers' 20th Century Dictionary*.)

Message, and regardeth it as the most meritorious of all deeds.[10] Here we have the essence of Bahá'í education.

A basis for infinite progress

In their Riḍván Message of 1972 the Universal House of Justice says:

... the laws, the religious obligations, the observances of Bahá'í life, Bahá'í moral principles and standards of dignity, decency and reverence, must become deeply implanted in Bahá'í consciousness and increasingly inform and characterize this community.[11]

If a thing is to become deeply implanted in the consciousness, one cannot start too soon on the process of getting it there. As with all attempts at human progress, one succeeds better before ideas have become set and habits fixed – that is, with the children. We must train our children from the beginning and hope that each generation will be more advanced than the last.

We need to ask ourselves what kind of adults we are hoping ultimately to produce. Let us remember that our journey is through all the worlds of God. We have never done with trying to improve ourselves. We can never say, 'I have arrived' and put 'B.A. Saintliness' after our names; nor are we presented, on arrival in the Abhá Kingdom, with our wings and halo done up neatly in a cellophane wrapper stamped 'Pure: a Bahá'í'.

Our training must be aimed at providing the basis for a journey whose progress, 'Abdu'l-Bahá tells us, is infinite towards God.* In other words, we need to lengthen our sights far beyond the goal of the fifteenth birthday; beyond even producing someone for whom the earth is but one country. Our vision must take in eternity – and this is some undertaking! Bahá'u'lláh says:

* See *Some Answered Questions*, Chapter 62.

O Son of Spirit! My first counsel is this: Possess a pure, kindly and radiant heart, that thine may be a sovereignty ancient, imperishable and everlasting.[12]

We need to help our children to understand the purpose *of* life and so give them a purpose *in* life. Our aim should be to produce those who are distinguished in that spiritual way to which 'Abdu'l-Bahá refers:

O army of God! Through the protection and help vouchsafed by the Blessed Beauty ye must conduct yourselves in such a manner that ye may stand out distinguished and brilliant as the sun among other souls. Should any one of you enter a city, he should become a centre of attraction by reason of his sincerity, his faithfulness and love, his honesty and fidelity, his truthfulness and loving-kindness towards all the peoples of the world, so that the people of that city may cry out and say: 'This man is unquestionably a Bahá'í, for his manners, his behaviour, his conduct, his morals, his nature and disposition reflect the attributes of the Bahá'ís.' Not until ye attain this station can ye be said to have been faithful to the Covenant and Testament of God.[13]

I desire distinction for you. The Bahá'ís must be distinguished from others of humanity. But this distinction must not depend upon wealth – that they should become more affluent than other people. I do not desire for you financial distinction. It is not an ordinary distinction I desire; not scientific, commercial, or industrial distinction. For you I desire spiritual distinction; that is, you must become eminent and distinguished in morals. In the love of God you must become distinguished from all else. You must become distinguished for loving humanity; for unity and accord; for love and justice. In brief, you must become distinguished in all the virtues of the human world; for faithfulness and sincerity; for justice and fidelity; for firmness and steadfastness; for philanthropic deeds and service to the human world; for love toward every human being; for unity and accord with all people; for removing prejudices and promoting international peace. Finally, you must become distinguished for heavenly illumination and acquiring the bestowals of God. I desire this distinction for you. This must be the point of distinction among you.[14]

The aim of an educator

'Abdu'l-Bahá tells us that

... the aim of an educator is to so train human souls that their angelic aspect may overcome their animal side.[15]

The Manifestations of God are the Divine Educators and Their Mission is

... to educate men, so that this piece of coal may become a diamond, and this fruitless tree may be engrafted and yield the sweetest, most delicious fruits.[16]

Unlike some educational theory, which refuses to face up to facts, 'Abdu'l-Bahá is never starry-eyed and unrealistic. He tells us quite definitely that people are different and have different capacities, and that these differences are innate:

The Manifestations of God ... affirm that differences are demonstrably and indisputably innate, and that 'We have caused some of you to excel others'* is a proven and inescapable fact. It is certain that human beings are, by their very nature, different one from the other. Observe a small group of children, born of the same parents, attending the same school, receiving the same education, living on the same diet: some, becoming well educated, will achieve a high degree of advancement; some will reach a middle level; and some will not prove educable at all. It is therefore clear that the disparity among individuals is due to differences of degree which are innate.[17]

Bahá'u'lláh Himself puts it vividly when He says,

The portion of some might lie in the palm of a man's hand, the

---
* Qur'án 17: 22

portion of others might fill a cup, and of others even a gallon-measure.[18]

However, 'Abdu'l-Bahá adds that the Manifestations of God 'also consider that training and education demonstrably exert a tremendous influence'.[19]

Here, in a chapter on education in general, we merely note the need for character training in passing and to do so does not imply any lack of emphasis. The Master gives it pride of place in the training of children and it is so supremely important that it will be dealt with in a chapter of its own (Chapter 3).

Three kinds of education

Education, the Master tells us, is of three kinds: material, human and spiritual.[20] All three are necessary but the third is the most important. He tells us that 'the most precious of gifts is attainment unto His [God's] unfailing guidance' and that the attainment of this 'is dependent upon knowledge and wisdom, and on being informed as to the mysteries of the Holy Words'.[21] Bahá'u'lláh says:

> Strain every nerve to acquire both inner and outer perfections, for the fruit of the human tree hath ever been and will ever be perfections both within and without.[22]

Note the word 'strain'.

In *Epistle to the Son of the Wolf* He says,

> ... knowledge is a veritable treasure for man, and a source of glory, of bounty, of joy, of exaltation, of cheer and gladness unto him. Happy the man that cleaveth unto it, and woe betide the heedless.[23]

What a delightful, inspiring way to look at knowledge and what an incentive to acquire it!

A word of warning

Bahá'u'lláh does, however, utter a word of warning which we should heed right at the start:

> Arts, crafts and sciences uplift the world of being, and are conducive to its exaltation. Knowledge is as wings to man's life, and a ladder for his ascent. Its acquisition is incumbent upon everyone. The knowledge of such sciences, however, should be acquired as can profit the peoples of the earth, and not those which begin with words and end with words.[24]

> This Day ... hath never been, nor is it now, the Day whereon man-made arts and sciences can be regarded as a true standard for men, since it hath been recognized that He Who was wholly unversed in any of them hath ascended the throne of purest gold, and occupied the seat of honor in the council of knowledge, whilst the acknowledged exponent and repository of these arts and sciences remained utterly deprived.[25]

Though He addresses the following remarks to the clergy, they are still valid for the rest of us:

> Weigh not the Book of God with such standards and sciences as are current amongst you, for the Book itself is the unerring balance established amongst men. In this most perfect balance whatsoever the peoples and kindreds of the earth possess must be weighed, while the measure of its weight should be tested according to its own standard, did ye but know it.[26]

Those who are tempted to judge everything at the bar of their own ideas and experience may find this hard to accept; but the Manifestation of God has all knowledge because of Who He is. Bahá'u'lláh says:

> The door of the knowledge of the Ancient Being hath ever been, and will continue for ever to be, closed in the face of men. No man's understanding shall ever gain access unto His holy court. As a token of His mercy, however, and as a proof of His loving-kindness, He hath manifested unto men the Day Stars of

His divine guidance, the Symbols of His divine unity, and hath ordained the knowledge of these sanctified Beings to be identical with the knowledge of His own Self. Whoso recognizeth them hath recognized God. Whoso hearkeneth to their call, hath hearkened to the Voice of God, and whoso testifieth to the truth of their Revelation, hath testified to the truth of God Himself. Whoso turneth away from them, hath turned away from God, and whoso disbelieveth in them, hath disbelieved in God. Every one of them is the Way of God that connecteth this world with the realms above, and the Standard of His Truth unto everyone in the kingdoms of earth and heaven. They are the Manifestations of God amidst men, the evidences of His Truth, and the signs of His glory.[27]

This being the case, we can accept what He says with confidence and this is the point from which we begin our children's education.

2

The Education of Children

A sacred duty

The attainment of education, then, is a command enjoined upon everyone, particularly Divine education – that brought by the Manifestation of God. We must *all* strive to attain both inner and outer perfections; but we have a sacred duty laid upon us as parents and that is to educate the children. Bahá'u'lláh commands it:

> We prescribe unto all men that which will lead to the exaltation of the Word of God amongst His servants, and likewise, to the advancement of the world of being and the uplift of souls. To this end, the greatest means is education of the child. To this must each and all hold fast. We have verily laid this charge upon you in manifold Tablets as well as in My Most Holy Book.* Well is it with him who deferreth thereto.[1]

> The Pen of Glory counselleth everyone regarding the instruction and education of children . . . Unto every father hath been enjoined the instruction of his son and daughter in the art of reading and writing and in all that hath been laid down in the Holy Tablet. He that putteth away that which is commanded unto him, the Trustees are then to take from him that which is required for their instruction, if he be wealthy, and if not the matter devolveth upon the House of Justice. Verily, have We made it a shelter for the poor and needy. He that bringeth up his

---

* The *Kitáb-i-Aqdas*

son or the son of another, it is as though he hath brought up a son of Mine; upon him rest My Glory, My Loving-Kindness, My Mercy, that have compassed the world.[2]

We are left in no doubt by the Master as to the paramount importance of obeying this command and the dire consequences, especially for the children, if we neglect it:

> The beloved of God and the maidservants of the Merciful must train their children with life and heart and teach them in the school of virtue and perfection. They must not be lax in this matter; they must not be inefficient. Truly, if a babe did not live at all it were better than to let it grow ignorant, for that innocent babe, in later life, would become afflicted with innumerable defects, responsible to and questioned by God, reproached and rejected by the people. What a sin this would be and what an omission![3]

The order of such education is important:

> As to the children: We have directed that in the beginning they should be trained in the observances and laws of religion: and thereafter, in such branches of knowledge as are of benefit, and in commercial pursuits that are distinguished for integrity, and in deeds that will further the victory of God's Cause or will attract some outcome which will draw the believer closer to his Lord.[4]

'Abdu'l-Bahá has a great deal to say on the subject. One paragraph will suffice at this point:

> ... it behoveth thee to nurture them at the breast of the love of God, and urge them onward to the things of the spirit, that they may turn their faces unto God; that their ways may conform to the rules of good conduct and their character be second to none; that they make their own all the graces and praiseworthy qualities of humankind; acquire a sound knowledge of the various branches of learning, so that from the very beginning of life they may become spiritual beings, dwellers in the Kingdom,

enamoured of the sweet breaths of holiness, and may receive an education religious, spiritual, and of the Heavenly Realm.[5]

The education of girls

One of the most revolutionary of all the teachings of the Bahá'í Faith is concerned with this very question of educating children. We are told that boys and girls should be treated alike in the matter of their education but if there *is* to be any preference, it must be given to the girls. 'Abdu'l-Bahá explains it thus:

> The first duty of the beloved of God and the maid-servants of the Merciful is this: they must strive by all possible means to educate both sexes, male and female; girls like boys; there is no difference whatsoever between them. The ignorance of both is blameworthy, and negligence in both cases is reprovable. 'Are they who know and they who do not know equal?'*
>
> The command is decisive concerning both. If it be considered through the eye of reality the training and culture of daughters is more necessary than that of sons, for these girls will come to the station of motherhood and will mold the lives of the children. The first trainer of the child is the mother. The babe, like unto a green and tender branch, will grow according to the way it is trained. If the training be right, it will grow right, and if crooked, the growth likewise, and unto the end of life it will conduct itself accordingly.
>
> Hence, it is firmly established that an untrained and uneducated daughter, on becoming a mother, will be the prime factor in the deprivation, ignorance, negligence and the lack of training of many children.
>
> O ye beloved of God and the maid-servants of the Merciful! Teaching and learning, according to the decisive texts of the Blessed Beauty (Bahá'u'lláh), is a duty. Whosoever is indifferent therein depriveth himself of the great bounty. Beware! Beware! that ye fail not in this matter. Endeavor with heart, with life, to

* *Qur'án* 39: 12

train your children, especially the daughters. No excuse is acceptable in this matter.⁶

To give preference to girls in families where the financial situation is such that choice has to be made is quite the opposite of all traditional thinking. To most people, even today, this is hard to swallow in practice, although they may see the sense of it in theory; but anyone who works in the social services will know that maternal deprivation is one of the root causes of family problems; and it is regrettably true that the 'iniquity of the fathers' is visited upon the children 'unto the third and fourth generation'.⁷ Just to give one example of this: a child who has been deprived of his mother's love when small, will be unable to give love in his turn and so the sad cycle passes on from one generation to another. Hasten the day when our wonderful teachings will have permeated society from top to bottom, for then we shall assuredly begin to breed a new race of men! 'Abdu'l-Bahá says:

> If, as she ought, the mother possesseth the learning and accomplishments of humankind, her children, like unto angels, will be fostered in all excellence, in right conduct and beauty.⁸

> If the mother is educated then her children will be well taught. When the mother is wise, then will the children be led into the path of wisdom. If the mother be religious she will show her children how they should love God. If the mother is moral she guides her little ones into the ways of uprightness.⁹

Some of His instructions are addressed to teachers in schools but they apply equally well to the home, and it is interesting to read what He says:

> Ye who are the teachers thereof must devote more of your efforts to character training than instruction, and must raise up your girl children to be modest and chaste, of good character

THE EDUCATION OF CHILDREN 15

and conduct – and in addition must teach them the various branches of knowledge.[10]

And further, those present should concern themselves with every means of training the girl children; with teaching the various branches of knowledge, good behaviour, a proper way of life, the cultivation of a good character, chastity and constancy, perseverance, strength, determination, firmness of purpose; with household management, the education of children, and whatever especially applieth to the needs of girls – to the end that these girls, reared in the stronghold of all perfections, and with the protection of a goodly character, will, when they themselves become mothers, bring up their children from earliest infancy to have a good character and conduct themselves well.[11]

Girls should be taught 'spiritual ethics and holy ways'[12] and also to

. . . study whatever will nurture the health of the body and its physical soundness, and how to guard their children from disease.

When matters are thus well arranged, every child will become a peerless plant in the gardens of the Abhá Paradise.[13]

. . . girls ought to be trained in such a manner that from day to day they will become more self-effacing, more humble, and will defer to and obey their parents and forebears, and be a comfort and a solace to all.[14]

Taken in conjunction with everything else that 'Abdu'l-Bahá says about the education of girls, this last paragraph can never be misunderstood as a reactionary statement. A girl can be well educated and take her rightful place in society and be all the things the Master desires as well.

Complementary responsibilities

It will be seen from the quotations included in the previous two sections that, whereas the responsibility for the early training of the children is given to the mother, it is the responsibility of the father to see to their formal education. We do not know how education will be organised in a Bahá'í world and I have sometimes wondered if Bahá'u'lláh's command to every father to 'instruct' his sons and daughters 'in the art of reading and writing' (interesting that *each* is described as an 'art') 'and in all that hath been laid down in the Holy Tablet'[15] means that he must literally do it himself; for a school curriculum will include a great many more subjects than this. Whatever it means, the point is clear: that the father must be responsible. This is logical in the light of the following passage from a letter written by the Universal House of Justice and included in their compilation *Family Life*:

... it can be inferred from a number of the responsibilities placed upon him, that the father can be regarded as the 'head' of the family. The members of a family all have duties and responsibilities towards one another and to the family as a whole, and these duties and responsibilities vary from member to member because of their natural relationships. The parents have the inescapable duty to educate their children – but not vice versa; the children have the duty to obey their parents – the parents do not obey the children; the mother – not the father – bears the children, nurses them in babyhood, and is thus their first educator, hence daughters have a prior right to education over sons and, as the Guardian's secretary has written on his behalf, 'The task of bringing up a Bahá'í child, as emphasized time and again in Bahá'í Writings, is the chief responsibility of the mother, whose unique privilege is indeed to create in her home such conditions as would be most conducive to both his material and spiritual welfare and advancement. The training which the child first receives through his mother constitutes the strongest foundation for his future development.' A corollary of this responsibility of the mother is her right to be supported by her husband – a husband has no explicit right to be supported by his wife. This principle of the husband's responsibility to provide for and protect the family can be seen applied also in the law of intestacy which provides that the family's dwelling place passes, on the father's death, not to his widow, but to his eldest son; the son at the same time has the responsibility to care for his mother.[16]

The one whose responsibility it is to support his wife and children must surely be made responsible for seeing that these same children receive a formal education. Exactly what Bahá'u'lláh means when He says that any father who fails to do this forfeits his rights of fatherhood remains to be seen, but the very fact that He can say such a thing only emphasises further the tremendous importance He lays upon the father's responsibility in this matter.

The long letter of the Universal House of Justice from which the above extract is taken should, I feel, be read in its entirety, and you will find the full text in the Appendix.

Children must exert themselves

But education is not just the responsibility of the parents. The children, too, must make an effort. Bahá'u'lláh says:

> It is incumbent upon the children to exert themselves to the utmost in acquiring the art of reading and writing. Writing skills that will provide for urgent needs will be enough for some; and then it is better and more fitting that they should spend their time in studying those branches of knowledge which are of use.
>
> As for what the Supreme Pen hath previously set down, the reason is that in every art and skill, God loveth the highest perfection.[17]

'Strive' – 'exert' – these are the words used by Bahá'u'lláh and 'Abdu'l-Bahá. Education and training are not to be had on a plate. Simone Weil, in an essay on the subject, says that the real purpose of education is to learn to apply oneself:

> Although people seem to be unaware of it today, the development of the faculty of attention forms the real object and almost the sole interest of studies.[18]

This is the crux of the matter; for if we are unwilling to make an effort we never get anywhere in anything, least of all in progressing along the spiritual path. 'Abdu'l-Bahá says:

> Thus shall they learn perseverance in all things, the will to advance, high mindedness and high resolve, chastity and purity of life. Thus shall they be enabled to carry to a successful conclusion whatsoever they undertake.[19]

The ultimate aim of education must always be before us. Bahá'u'lláh says:

> At the outset of every endeavour, it is incumbent to look to the end of it. Of all the arts and sciences, set the children to studying those which will result in advantage to man, will ensure his progress and elevate his rank. Thus the noisome odours of lawlessness will be dispelled, and thus through the high endeavours of the nation's leaders, all will live cradled, secure and in peace.[20]

To comment on the scholastic aspect of this would be out of place here; but education in the home still has an objective. If we are wise, we shall 'look to the end of it'. Our long-term aim must surely be to light the spark of faith in our children's hearts so that they will grow up to serve God and humanity with all the ardour that is in them; and that they, in their turn, will hand this torch of faith on to their own children.

3

Character Training

A hard task

Let us not imagine, however, that our task as parents is easy. It is not. Indeed, as an elderly friend of my husband remarked to us when our twins were a few months old, 'Ah, yes, the first twenty years are the worst.' As parents, we do take on a task of that length – sometimes longer. It is not just a Six Year Plan. As 'Abdu'l-Bahá says:

> It is . . . very difficult to undertake this service, even harder to succeed in it.[1]

He is actually talking to teachers in a Sunday School but it is useful advice for parents as well. Here is some more:

> If this activity is well organized, rest thou assured that it will yield great results. Firmness and steadfastness, however, are necessary, otherwise it will continue for some time, but later be gradually forgotten. Perseverance is an essential condition. In every project firmness and steadfastness will undoubtedly lead to good results; otherwise it will exist for some days, and then be discontinued.[2]

Of course, one's family does not disappear after a course of lessons, nor can one forget them, but the point about firmness, steadfastness and perseverance is extremely relevant to parents. Unless we are firm, steadfast and persevering, say, in the inculcation of the habit of morning and evening reading and prayer, it will be only too easy to let it drop when pressures such as homework begin to develop and at least one parent wants to go to bed before it is finished.

The work of bringing up a family is the hardest, most demanding but also the most satisfying and rewarding job that anyone can undertake and one to which parents should be prepared to devote a substantial portion of their lives. One cannot bring children up as a side-line. They are a full-time job. When our children are born we embark upon a Twenty-one Year Plan for each one of them. Family life has to be worked at; yet it is the one job for which we are the least prepared. We expect to need training in anything else we do as a job – and sometimes even as a hobby. Surely parenthood and family life deserve at least an equal preparation? I should like to see a course or courses on this subject, perhaps prepared by a special committee of the National Spiritual Assembly. It would be based firmly on the Writings and would cover every aspect of the raising of a family in far greater detail than is within the scope of this book. It would not only deal with the psychological side of things, but with children's health and hygiene, food and drink – indeed, everything the committee could think of. I am sure that such guidance would be immensely helpful, for without it the attitudes, thinking and behaviour of the outside world will influence, willy nilly, the attitudes, thinking and behaviour of our young people.

No other job in the world is as important as raising a family and we enter into it supremely confident of our ability to make a good job of it. When our children have grown up we may be able to see whether or not this confidence was justified, but that is a rather hit-and-miss way of going on. It is surely better to prepare ourselves for it with some preliminary study and thought. As has already been said, 'Abdu'l-Bahá makes it quite clear that the most important aspect of education is character training, so we will start there.

Three kinds of character

Before one can embark successfully on character training, it is useful to know what one is dealing with. 'Abdu'l-Bahá tells us that there are three kinds of character: innate, inherited and acquired.[3]

Innate character concerns differences of degree: one's natural capacity – what God gave one, if you like.

> . . . it is clear that in the original nature there exists a difference of degree and varieties of worthiness and capacity. This difference does not imply good or evil but is simply a difference of degree.[4]

One's latent capacity, being God-given, is *there*; it is fixed – a fact one must accept and be grateful for. As with the parable of the talents,[5] one must make the best of one's endowments and not complain because one hasn't as many as somebody else. In other words, we should always take the positive line with our children and try to bring out – and encourage them to develop – the gifts they have.

Inherited character comes from strength or weakness of constitution: as with parents, so with children. As I see it, this can best be improved by each succeeding generation growing up in the Faith and letting it – the Faith – become deeply implanted in their consciousness. One can also improve one's own constitution and that of one's children and descendants by paying attention to correct eating habits and a healthy way of life – but that is another subject!

Acquired character is very important and is the aspect

with which education is most concerned. Bahá'u'lláh says:

> Man is the supreme Talisman.* Lack of a proper education hath, however, deprived him of that which he doth inherently possess. Through a word proceeding out of the mouth of God he was called into being; by one word more he was guided to recognize the Source of his education; by yet another word his station and destiny were safeguarded. The Great Being saith: Regard man as a mine rich in gems of inestimable value. Education can, alone, cause it to reveal its treasures, and enable mankind to benefit therefrom.[6]

Character can become saintly or depraved, according to how it is educated. 'Abdu'l-Bahá uses the example of a man gradually accustoming himself to take poison, such as opium, so that in time he becomes so addicted to it that he cannot do without it. His comments on the difference between purity in a child and purity in a man are also very interesting:

> The hearts of all children are of the utmost purity. They are mirrors upon which no dust has fallen. But this purity is on account of weakness and innocence, not on account of any strength and testing, for as this is the early period of their childhood, their hearts and minds are unsullied by the world. They cannot display any great intelligence. They have neither hypocrisy nor deceit. This is on account of the child's weakness, whereas the man becomes pure through his strength. Through the power of intelligence he becomes simple; through the great power of reason and understanding and not through the power of weakness he becomes sincere.[7]

The teacher as doctor

The teacher – in this case the parent – has also to be a doctor to the child's character:

---

* Talisman: an object supposed to be endued with magical powers; a charm. Hence man has inherent powers superior to any ordinary talisman.

that is, he must, in instructing the child, remedy its faults; must give him learning, and at the same time rear him to have a spiritual nature . . . For the inner reality of man is a demarcation line between the shadow and the light . . . With education it can achieve all excellence; devoid of education it will stay on, at the lowest point of imperfection.⁸*

In other words, we should train our children to become, and also try ourselves to be, those 'steadfast, self-sacrificing individuals' whom the Universal House of Justice so much wants to see.⁹

Love for God and for His Manifestation

In this the first, indeed the only, firm basis for progress, is love for and faith in God and His Manifestation and obedience to Their will – that is, firmness in the Covenant. Bahá'u'lláh talks of the twofold obligation to remain steadfast in His love and to observe strictly the laws He has given to us; but before love comes recognition, because you cannot love what you do not know:

> The first duty prescribed by God for His servants is the recognition of Him Who is the Day Spring of His Revelation and the Fountain of His laws, Who representeth the Godhead in both the Kingdom of His Cause and the world of creation. Whoso achieveth this duty hath attained unto all good; and whoso is deprived thereof, hath gone astray, though he be the author of every righteous deed. It behoveth every one who reacheth this most sublime station, this summit of transcendent glory, to observe every ordinance of Him Who is the Desire of the world. These twin duties are inseparable. Neither is acceptable without the other. Thus hath it been decreed by Him Who is the Source of Divine inspiration.¹⁰

Love for God is the only true foundation for faith and the

---

* See *Some Answered Questions*, ch. 81 pp. 285–6 (USA 1981) for 'Abdu'l-Bahá's comments on the arc of ascent and descent.

only thing that will see us through in time of trouble. 'Abdu'l-Bahá says:

> Thanks be to God that thou hast obtained that which was sought by all prophets and holy saints; namely, the knowledge of God and the love of God. First, the knowledge; and, second, His unfathomable love . . . This is a great gift from God and hath no equal; although, in this physical world, its greatness is not perceivable, nor its nature clearly known, yet, in the spiritual world, it shineth like the sun.[11]

There is an order in the development of this relationship to God and this is what we as parents should try to pass on to our children: first knowledge, then love, faith, obedience and finally steadfastness. Of steadfastness Bahá'u'lláh says:

> this can in no wise be attained except through full recognition of Him; and full recognition cannot be obtained save by faith in the blessed words: 'He doeth whatsoever He willeth.' Whoso tenaciously cleaveth unto this sublime word and drinketh deep from the living waters of utterance which are inherent therein, will be imbued with such a constancy that all the books of the world will be powerless to deter him from the Mother Book.* O how glorious is this sublime station, this exalted rank, this ultimate purpose![12]

If we manage to help our children to obtain this gift from God, then we have given them the most precious help this human life can bestow.

The fear of God

Before we can start doing anything we need to have some conception of the nature of man and what a precious gem of God's mine we are dealing with. The aim is to pass

---

* *Ummu'l-Kitáb*, the Mother Book, the heavenly original of the Scriptures which are revealed to the Manifestations of God. Cf. *Qur'án* 3: 5 and 43: 3.

beyond personality to become a channel for the uninterrupted flow of His grace to mankind:

> From among all created things He hath singled out for His special favour the pure, the gem-like reality of man, and invested it with a unique capacity of knowing Him and of reflecting the greatness of His glory.[13]

> Souls are like unto mirrors, and the bounty of God is like unto the sun. When the mirrors pass beyond all coloring and attain purity and polish, and are confronted with the sun, they will reflect in full perfection its light and glory. In this condition one should not consider the mirror, but the power of the light of the sun, which hath penetrated the mirror, making it a reflector of the heavenly glory.[14]

We need to understand that

> The fear of God hath ever been the prime factor in the education of His creatures. Well is it with them that have attained thereunto![15]

What is meant by the fear of God is a question which we might well consider, but it is too big a subject to go into in any detail here. Briefly, I think it is intended as a positive quality, not an abject terror, and has to do with the recognition of our total dependence on God and the apprehension of the fact that if He ceased to love us, we would cease to exist. Bahá'u'lláh says:

> That which is of paramount importance for the children, that which must precede all else, is to teach them the oneness of God and the Laws of God. For lacking this, the fear of God cannot be inculcated, and lacking the fear of God an infinity of odious and abominable actions will spring up, and sentiments will be uttered that transgress all bounds . . .
> The parents must exert every effort to rear their offspring to be religious, for should the children not attain this greatest of adornments, they will not obey their parents, which in a certain sense means that they will not obey God. Indeed, such children

will show no consideration to anyone, and will do exactly as they please.¹⁶

The Guardian says:

> In explaining the fear of God to children, there is no objection to teaching it as 'Abdu'l-Bahá so often taught everything, in the form of parables. Also the child should be made to understand that we don't fear God because He is cruel, but we fear Him because He is just, and, if we do wrong and deserve to be punished, then in His justice He may see fit to punish us. We must both love God and fear Him.¹⁷

> You ask him about the fear of God: perhaps the friends do not realize that the majority of human beings need the element of fear in order to discipline their conduct? Only a relatively very highly evolved soul would always be disciplined by love alone. Fear of punishment, fear of the anger of God if we do evil, are needed to keep people's feet on the right path. Of course we should love God – but we must fear Him in the sense of a child fearing the righteous anger and chastisement of a parent; not cringe before Him as before a tyrant, but know His mercy exceeds His justice!¹⁸

Basic spiritual laws

There are certain basic spiritual laws which we have to teach our children, for without them nothing can be achieved: truthfulness and trustworthiness; justice, with its need for moderation and self-defence; respect for and consideration of others, which are the foundation of good manners; obedience, self-discipline, kindness and so on; but by far the most important is truthfulness.

Truthfulness and trustworthiness

'Abdu'l-Bahá goes so far as to say

> Truthfulness is the foundation of all the virtues of the world

of humanity. Without truthfulness, progress and success in all of the worlds of God are impossible for a soul. When this holy attribute is established in man, all the divine qualities will also become realized.[19]

Truthfulness is more than just telling the truth: it is *living* it. Truthfulness and trustworthiness are the verbal and practical sides of the coin of integrity. Integrity means 'entireness, wholeness: the unimpaired state of anything: uprightness: honesty: purity'.[20] It comes from Latin roots which mean 'not' and 'touch'. In other words, one is not touchable, one cannot be corrupted.

Recently I heard a Bahá'í friend say, 'The letters of the Universal House of Justice are written in response to specific situations but their compilations are anticipatory.' If we look back at the titles of these compilations, we will realise that this is true: they do anticipate a need and we should do well to ask ourselves what the House is trying to tell us. As the Bahá'í friend then went on to point out, the latest one (1987) is on 'Trustworthiness'. So for this reason as well as the fact that truthfulness and trustworthiness are the foundation of all virtues, we will go into the subject with some thoroughness.

One can see why truthfulness and trustworthiness are the most fundamental of all human virtues. Once a person has lost his good name by lying or deceit he will find it extremely difficult, if not impossible, to regain it. Once a person has stolen someone else's property, be it at school or at work or wherever it is, he is the first person to be suspected next time something is missing. In His Tablet to Sulṭán 'Abdu'l-Azíz Bahá'u'lláh links these virtues with belief in God:

> Know thou for a certainty that whoso disbelieveth in God is neither trustworthy nor truthful. This indeed is the truth, the undoubted truth. He that acteth treacherously towards God will

also act treacherously towards his king. Nothing whatever can deter such a man from evil, nothing can hinder him from betraying his neighbour, nothing can induce him to walk uprightly.[21]

This is one of Bahá'u'lláh's startling statements – what Christ's disciples called 'a hard saying';[22] but if you think about it, it is true. If you don't believe in God, why should you be truthful or trustworthy? If you don't believe in God, it follows that you feel no compelling need to live according to His teachings. There are, of course, many people who call themselves atheists or humanists who lead very good lives and whose morals are not in question; but such people, while denying the Source of their moral standards with their lips, do, in fact, live out the teachings of the Manifestations of God in their lives. The weakness of this position is that one is living, as it were, on spiritual capital and in time that capital will all be used up. In an increasingly materialistic society, based on acquisitiveness and self-advancement, it needs something stronger, a more powerful motive, than just 'natural law', or whatever other man-made philosophy one may use as a guide for moral behaviour, to induce us to walk uprightly. Without the sanctions and restraints of religion on the one hand and its positive teachings on the other, sooner or later morals will crack. Without God's command 'Thou shalt' (or 'Thou shalt not', as the case may be) to pass on to our children, they will inevitably be influenced by selfishness, a desire to be popular and so on. If our children are not to retreat before the onslaught of lowering moral standards, of whatever kind, we must train them rigorously to be truthful and trustworthy. This is not the place to embark on a lengthy treatise on the subject. Suffice it to say that without these two virtues it is obvious that the whole of society would become unstable and eventually collapse.

We need to teach our children to be absolutely honest and trustworthy in everything, however insignificant it may be: that if they make a promise, they must keep it; that they must fulfil their obligations – and conversely, they must not promise that which they do not fulfil;[23] that they must always tell the truth and do the right thing for the love of God and because it is right, not because they are afraid of being 'found out' and punished.

I should like to emphasise this point. Some religious teaching in the past has used the threat of the torment of hell-fire as a way of keeping its followers from sinning. If they wouldn't keep on the straight and narrow for the love of God, then they must be made to keep on it for fear of eternal damnation. I have always found this idea utterly repugnant and the relish with which some writers have gone into detail about the nature of the fate awaiting these unfortunate sinners can only be described as sadistic. Reward and punishment *are* elements in the upbringing of children – and indeed in the running of society – but I do not believe that this picture of God is either inspiring or true to Bahá'í teaching. If we develop our children's consciences at a tender age, the mere knowledge that they have done something wrong will be enough. Surely it is far better to instil into their young hearts a devotion to God as their Heavenly Father and a desire to please Him by doing His will, than to give the impression that He is a kind of glorified old-fashioned headmaster with a cane poised ready to administer pain for every peccadillo. We have already dealt with the meaning of 'the fear of God' and that it is not to be thought of as an abject, cringing terror. The Báb expresses vividly the point we have been discussing in the following passage:

Worship thou God in such wise that if thy worship lead thee to the fire, no alteration in thine adoration would be produced, and so likewise if thy recompense should be paradise. Thus and thus alone should be the worship which befitteth the one True God. Shouldst thou worship Him because of fear, this would be unseemly in the sanctified Court of His presence, and could not be regarded as an act by thee dedicated to the Oneness of His Being. Or if thy gaze should be on paradise, and thou shouldst worship Him while cherishing such a hope, thou wouldst make God's creation a partner with Him, notwithstanding the fact that paradise is desired by men.

Fire and paradise both bow down and prostrate themselves before God. That which is worthy of His Essence is to worship Him for His sake, without fear of fire, or hope of paradise.

Although when true worship is offered, the worshipper is delivered from the fire, and entereth the paradise of God's good-pleasure, yet such should not be the motive of his act. However, God's favour and grace ever flow in accordance with the exigencies of His inscrutable wisdom.

The most acceptable prayer is the one offered with the utmost spirituality and radiance; its prolongation hath not been and is not beloved by God. The more detached and the purer the prayer, the more acceptable is it in the presence of God.[24]

In daily life there are many occasions when 'white lies' are indulged in so as not to hurt people's feelings. I believe that even this is a dangerous practice and that it is perfectly possible to phrase one's remarks in such a way that one neither hurts people's feelings nor tells a falsehood. We are bidden to be guarded in our speech.[25] So, when somebody gives you a present you don't like, you don't apply honesty in the other direction and immediately blurt out that you don't like it, but exclaim, 'Oh, how kind of you!' or some such inoffensive comment – because that, at least, is true: it *was* kind of the person to give you the present. It is the divine *art*, not science, of living.

'Abdu'l-Bahá puts it very strongly indeed when He says,

The individual must be educated to such a high degree that he would rather have his throat cut than tell a lie, and would think it easier to be slashed with a sword or pierced with a spear than to utter calumny or be carried away by wrath.[26]

If we can imagine the frightful physical pain involved in submitting to either of these two alternatives, we may begin to appreciate the station of truthfulness – that the spiritual pain involved in departing from it would be so great that we preferred to be physically hurt. A new race of men indeed!

I have dealt so far with the positive side of this question: the training of our own children to be truthful and trustworthy. Now we must address ourselves to the negative side: that is, how we help our children to cope with the fact that *other people* are not always entirely truthful or trustworthy.

If you look into the eyes of a baby and see the complete innocence, openness and trust expressed in them, you feel you are looking straight into that infant's soul, pure and undefiled as it is at that age. You long for that innocence and trust to remain there always and feel how sad it is that at some future date that little child will have to learn how the world is and that not everyone is worthy of his trust. It should be the case that, as that baby develops into a toddler and small child, he should be able to go to anyone, trustingly and without fear. It is to be hoped that one day this will be possible; but at present, regrettably, it is not so. It has always been necessary to teach one's children not to talk to strangers or go with them; but today this has to be done at a lamentably tender age. With the spread of AIDS it has suddenly become very urgent. It is tragic that, because of the imperative need to protect our children in the modern world, they have to be made aware of dangers and of things they shouldn't have to know anything about until much older, at three and four years of age. It seems they are to be denied the right of every child to be a child and have a carefree, innocent childhood. However, we cannot ignore the present-day world and wish that our little children didn't have to know about it. In this country at any rate it is coming at them from hoardings, from the television and in school, and whether we like it or not they will hear about it. It is very much linked with the question of trustworthiness.

It seems to me that there are two aspects of the question of teaching our children that not everyone is trustworthy. One is that we have to explain this gradually to them and the other is that we ourselves must protect them by not allowing them to go out, either on their own or with other children, unless we ourselves, or another responsible older person is with them. We will discuss the second one first.

However many times our little girl of seven or eight may have come home from school successfully, this doesn't mean that there may not be an odd occasion when she will forget our instructions (even if she doesn't deliberately disobey them) and be persuaded to go off on some 'adventure' by a classmate before returning to her house. This could be the one time when disaster strikes and we are left with the guilt of not having fetched her ourselves.

So we ourselves, or a trusted friend or neighbour, will take the children to school and be there to meet them at the school gate when they come out. How long we go on doing this will depend on how far the school is from our home as well as how many roads there are to cross. It will also depend on whether we live in a small village or in a large town or city. If the latter, we should be wise to collect them for a much longer period than in a village, where the school may be only fifty yards down the road and *somebody* is probably watching the children as they go up the road, even if from behind lace curtains. Just as there comes a time when we allow each child in turn to cross a busy main road by herself, there also comes a time when we must trust her to go to and from school by herself. It has to be instilled into her that she must come *straight* home and not dawdle on the way or be tempted to go off somewhere with her friends, however attractive or safe it may seem to her to be.

When we allow the children to go to a friend's house to play, we should be sure that that child's mother or father or some other adult is present. Even in our own garden, where one would hope they would be safe, we should look out of the window from time to time to see that all is well.

For those families who only have a back yard or live in a flat where there is no garden whatsoever, there is obviously a difficulty. Children cannot be expected to have their freedom curtailed to that extent and not want to go and play somewhere where there is more room. Often, all that such children have to play in is the local park or on some patch of derelict land, either of which may be some way from their home. Fine – as long as somebody is with them. This may require a degree of organisation, either of our own day or in planning a 'Mums' rota', so that we ourselves or someone else is there keeping an eye on them.

When I was a child it was safer to wander than it is today but still we were told, by whichever parent was with us, 'Don't get out of my sight.' This should be enough in normal circumstances even today; but the price of freedom for our children is eternal vigilance on our part. As they grow older and enter their teens, this vigilance will become increasingly unobtrusive but it should never be entirely withdrawn. We may not expect to meet our sixteen-year-old daughter from school (unless we have a car, which would be acceptable to her, as many parents do this and she wouldn't be made to feel a baby), but we can – and should – insist on her observing everything we have taught her. Children and young people are vulnerable in different ways at different stages and in the nature of things, girls are more at risk than boys. The places where one might expect to find solitude – leafy lanes and lonely moors – are often the very places where the greatest danger lies and our children and young people should be discouraged from being alone in places where nobody could hear them, no matter how loudly they screamed.

I have no recollection of how old I was when I was warned about not talking to strangers. In those days the question was largely theoretical in any case. I don't even remember how I introduced the idea to my own children. It was something one more or less grew up with. The skill has to be in warning them without giving them the idea that *nobody* is to be trusted. In my own case, I suspect it began when I was about four. We were staying for our summer holidays at a little place called West Runton on the Norfolk coast. On this particular afternoon, we had had our picnic tea on the beach and my two older brothers and I asked permission to go and paddle and make sand-castles before going 'home'. This granted, we went down to the water's edge amongst a number of other children. It was further down the beach than normal because we were nearing the period of the highest 'Spring Tide'. I suppose my parents thought my brothers could keep an eye on me. Having paddled about for a bit, I conceived the idea of walking to Cromer, a much larger seaside resort about four miles along the coast. So I set off – and nobody saw me go. It must have been about five o'clock and families were beginning to pack up and go back to their lodgings. I met nobody on my walk and proceeded quite happily until I reached Cromer. I was carrying my bucket and spade and had collected a tough beach grass on the way. I saw a sort of stone or concrete ramp with a balustrade going up from the beach to a raised concrete area with huts where people were sitting. I thought, 'I'll touch the end of that (meaning the balustrade – I wouldn't have known what to call it at that age) with my spade, the grass and my hand, and then I'll go home.' I did this, turned round and walked all the way back again. There was still nobody about and when I got back to being within sight of our row of tents, I saw that the beach was empty except for somebody who appeared to be waving at me. As I drew nearer, I was surprised to find it was a cousin of my mother who was on holiday with us. I waved back quite cheerfully and was amazed at the somewhat frantic, though not scolding, welcome I got. She took me by the hand and no doubt asked me where I had been, telling me that my parents had been very worried and had been looking for me everywhere. We found my mother at the top of the cliff and my amazement was increased tenfold when she fell on her knees, hugged me to herself and wept. I wondered what all the fuss was about. I had only been for a walk! We found my father, who was equally happy to see me though not so demonstrative, and I was taken home and put to bed as usual. Nothing more was said that night. Next morning I was summoned to my parents' bedroom. My mother was already up and she left me to climb into the bed beside my father, for him to explain to me the enormity of what I had done. They had had the coastguards out and the police and all sorts of people looking for me; how I had frightened them and so on. I don't remember anything being said about strangers but I daresay it was. What I do remember was the way my father handled it. He did not scold me as he would have done for some lesser offence. It was so serious that he explained my fault to me quietly but firmly, on my own away from my brothers, in a comfortable and loving setting, and made me promise that I would never do it again. Obtaining my co-operation and obedience in this way was far more effective than the ranting and smacking that some fathers would have meted out the minute the child reappeared.

Incidentally, the thing that *really* hurt my feelings about that little episode was that nobody would believe I had actually got as far as Cromer!

In this instance, there is absolutely no doubt that the parents were caring and responsible and did oversee their family in all circumstances. Yet even so, it was possible for a child to detach herself from the group and walk quite a distance along the beach until there was a bend and the headland hid her from view, and not be seen by anybody. Fortunately, nothing ill-toward happened on this occasion, for which one can only thank God; and I am sure my parents did – fervently.

But what of those who deliberately leave their children alone in the house, for whatever reason, especially after dark, no matter how early in the winter this may be. Some of the most horrific tragedies involving children occur because the parents are irresponsible – or even just not sufficiently awake to the dangers – in this matter of leaving children alone.

The possibility of our children being abducted or sexually assaulted are thankfully remote and may be less than a one-in-a-million chance. To find that a *parent* is untruthful or untrustworthy can be shattering for a child and has to be lived with every day. Even one fall from grace can be traumatic for a sensitive child. It was stated at the beginning of this book that there should be no double standard in the moral law and what we wouldn't do or say in front of the children, we shouldn't do or say at all. One of the instances given was the use of bad language. A lady whom I know very well had exactly this experience. She had been taught that it was wicked to swear, and for the first ten years of her life she never heard any swearing in her home at all. Then one day her father exclaimed 'Damn!' in front of her. Whether he was taken off his guard or whether he thought it was time she was introduced to the realities of life she never knew, but the effect was devastating. Her father tumbled off his pedestal and there began literally years of inner conflict for that child. It manifested itself in the development of migraine headaches (though she didn't connect the two until many years later). She never said a word to anyone about her distress but it affected her behaviour in several ways, the most obvious to her parents being that she became moody and was unhappy about something. It was not until she was fourteen that an inkling of this was disclosed. When her mother went upstairs to have their nightly prayers, she found her daughter in tears and she finally got it out of her that the trouble was her father. On being asked gently, 'Can't you go to him and talk it over?' she sobbed, 'No!' This incident was not the sole cause of the tension between her and her father but it was the beginning of it and it was at least another seven years before she could summon up enough courage to tell him about it – and there was a reconciliation. Compared to what some children suffer, you may think this was trivial; but it was far from trivial to that child to have her own father do the very thing he had taught her was wicked. It represented a betrayal of trust.

As for introducing our children verbally to the idea that not everyone can be trusted, we can probably accomplish this without too much difficulty, even in today's climate, if it has been made less necessary by our making sure that somebody is always with them. In other words, it is likely to be hypothetical rather than actual to begin with. It can be imbibed with stories – and I don't mean ones which deal specifically with such issues – which we shall read to them in the normal way we do read to children. Or we may find that something quite simple, like a workman promising to come and do a job for us on a certain date and then not turning up, provides an opportunity to talk about trustworthiness – without laying it on too thickly at this stage. We might come across a child on his own while taking ours for a walk. We shall probably want to ascertain that an adult companion is nearby or that his home is just over there and he is making straight for it. We can use such an occasion to explain to our own child why we think the other's Mummy should be with him: 'Well, you see, just *sometimes* there might be someone about who might be unkind and hurt him in some way, or kidnap him like the man in that story we read yesterday – do you remember?' The child no doubt will. 'And you know how terribly frightened Johnny and Susan were in that story, don't you? You wouldn't like anything like that to happen to you, would you?' The difficulties undergone by Johnny and Susan probably didn't contain the slightest suggestion of the kind of thing we are referring to; but they may well have been a little frightening to our child, even within the safety of our own arms, and they will be quite enough to make him understand that there are dangers in disobeying Mummy and Daddy and going off with strangers. Large round eyes and a long-drawn-out 'No-o-o!' shows that the child is taking it in. 'Then you won't ever go off with anybody, will you? It's better not to talk to strangers just in case they might turn out to be like the man in the story.'

However we tackle it, we don't want to turn our children into suspicious and unfriendly people. Once they understand that they must *never* go off with anyone with whom a specific arrangement has not been made (and they know about it), of course they can tell someone the time or show him the way (without going with him to show it). Precept – the positive instruction of our children in the Faith – will of course accompany this. One mother, having to cope with searching questions prompted by a talk at her children's school in which they were told not to let any grown-up try and make them do things they didn't want to do, said to her children, 'If you always remember to do what Bahá'u'lláh says, you will be all right.' This presupposes that her children *were* aware of the standards of the Faith.

Because of the increase in child abuse, there are now books on the market warning children of the dangers and meant for them to read to themselves. I have one in front of me now. The text is simple and the illustrations good in a straightforward way, not cartoony or horrific (this is right – it is not a joking matter). It portrays three or four situations and gives advice as to what the child should do if he finds himself caught up in one of them. Though it is well told, I think it is better if we as mothers sit down and read the book *with* our children. It could be frightening, even though in this particular book, published in association with the National Children's Home,* it is handled extremely well. From our point of view, however, the religious content is missing and we need to put the whole thing in the context of our Faith.

There is sometimes some confusion in our minds as to whether or not it is right for a Bahá'í child to tell even his parents about any unpleasant experience he may have had, because this constitutes backbiting. Any idea that such talk is backbiting and shouldn't be indulged in is very dangerous. 'Telling tales' about the little faults of classmates is one thing but telling parents or teacher or a policeman or policewoman about something frightening that happened to him is quite another. For one thing,

---

* A long-established and highly respected British children's charity.

withholding such information will not only result in possible mental and emotional disturbance for the child concerned, which could last for the rest of his life, but it will ensure that other people's children suffer in the same way.

If it be objected that all this is overdoing it a bit and that children must learn to stand on their own feet, I would say, Which is more important – that they should be well-protected and live to be *able* to stand on their own feet, or that they should be allowed to wander about without protection and run the risk of their dishonoured and mutilated little corpses being fished out of a river miles from home?

We can teach our children that we should all pray for such people – healing prayers for their hearts and souls, which are sick; that they be made aware of their sinning and come to repent of it; and when they have repented, that God will forgive them – for repentance must precede forgiveness, otherwise that forgiveness is meaningless; and that they will resolve to live a new and wholesome life in future. We can forgive them personally but society is built upon justice and not upon forgiveness and they will have to be punished in whatever way that society thinks best.

Most examples of untruthfulness or untrustworthiness are not as serious as those we have been talking about and we have to instil into our children the idea that, even if others sometimes tell a fib or let them down, they must never do either of these things. Here, the rule of not telling tales, or 'splitting', to use a schoolboy term, is one that should be upheld as far as is possible, along with the honourable 'owning up' which is a corollary of that schoolboy rule (and schoolgirl, of course!). Each set of parents has to decide for themselves what they consider to be backbiting and discouraged and what to be very necessary information, not just for their own child's protection, but for the protection of society as well.

Justice

Bahá'u'lláh says:

> O people of God! That which traineth the world is Justice, for it is upheld by two pillars, reward and punishment. These two pillars are the sources of life to the world.[27]

He also says that schools should

> first train the children in the principles of religion, so that the Promise and the Threat recorded in the Books of God may prevent them from the things forbidden and adorn them with the mantle of the commandments; but this in such a measure that it may not injure the children by resulting in ignorant fanaticism and bigotry.[28]

As we said earlier, what goes for schools can also go for parents. We probably have very little conception yet of what Bahá'u'lláh means when He talks about justice. Perhaps true justice is not that one treats everybody in exactly the same way but that, circumstances being different and characters and capacities unequal, justice should also be unequal.

Perhaps the most fundamental conception of justice which our children are capable of understanding in their early years is the application of the Golden Rule – 'Do unto others as you would that they should do unto you'; but there is another way of looking at justice which might throw some light on Bahá'u'lláh's statement that it is 'the best-beloved of all things'[29] in God's sight. Christ told His followers to forgive anyone who did them harm and to repay injury with double kindness:

> Ye have heard that it hath been said, An eye for an eye, and a tooth for a tooth:

But I say unto you, That ye resist not evil: but whosoever shall smite thee on thy right cheek, turn to him the other also.

And, if any man will sue thee at the law, and take away thy coat, let him have *thy* cloke also.

And whosoever shall compel thee to go a mile, go with him twain.

Give to him that asketh thee, and from him that would borrow of thee turn not thou away.

Ye have heard that it hath been said, Thou shalt love thy neighbour, and hate thine enemy.

But I say unto you, Love your enemies, bless them that curse you, do good to them that hate you, and pray for them which despitefully use you, and persecute you.[30]

Indeed, the phrase 'to turn the other cheek' has entered into the language and is probably one of the best known of Christ's ethical teachings. Here, the emphasis is on forgiveness. His followers must *love* their enemies. 'Abdu'l-Bahá says the same thing:

Should other peoples and nations be unfaithful to you show your fidelity unto them, should they be unjust toward you show justice towards them, should they keep aloof from you attract them to yourself, should they show their enmity be friendly towards them, should they poison your lives sweeten their souls, should they inflict a wound upon you be a salve to their sores. Such are the attributes of the sincere! Such are the attributes of the truthful.[31]

But this is the standard of behaviour between individuals. It would not work for society as a whole. As soon as a third party enters into the situation, *justice* becomes necessary. It can therefore be seen, in this context, as love applied to the group. 'Abdu'l-Bahá explains it thus:

when Christ said: 'Whosoever shall smite thee on the right cheek, turn to him the left one also,' it was for the purpose of teaching men not to take personal revenge. He did not mean that, if a wolf should fall upon a flock of sheep and wish to destroy it, the wolf should be encouraged to do so. No, if Christ had known that a wolf had entered the fold and was about to destroy the sheep, most certainly He would have prevented it.

As forgiveness is one of the attributes of the Merciful One, so also justice is one of the attributes of the Lord. The tent of existence is upheld upon the pillar of justice and not upon forgiveness. The continuance of mankind depends upon justice and not upon forgiveness. So if, at present, the law of pardon were practiced in all countries, in a short time the world would be disordered, and the foundations of human life would crumble.

To recapitulate: the constitution of the communities depends upon justice, not upon forgiveness. Then what Christ meant by forgiveness and pardon is not that, when nations attack you, burn your homes, plunder your goods, assault your wives, children and relatives, and violate your honor, you should be submissive in the presence of these tyrannical foes and allow them to perform all their cruelties and oppressions. No, the words of Christ refer to the conduct of two individuals toward each other: if one person assaults another, the injured one should forgive him. But the communities must protect the rights of man. So if someone assaults, injures, oppresses and wounds me, I will offer no resistance, and I will forgive him. But if a person wishes to assault Siyyid Manshadí,* certainly I will prevent him. Although for the malefactor noninterference is apparently a kindness, it would be an oppression to Manshadí. If at this moment a wild Arab were to enter this place with a drawn sword, wishing to assault, wound and kill you, most assuredly I would prevent him. If I abandoned you to the Arab, that would not be justice but injustice. But if he injure me personally, I would forgive him.[32]

In so far as the family is a little community, this idea of justice as love applied to the group is relevant, as is also forgiveness. Examples of both these two aspects of

---

* A Bahá'í sitting with the group at table.

relationships abound every single day. If one of our children does something which is reprehensible on an individual level, such as being disobedient, rude or unkind to us personally, while not overlooking the correction (and possibly punishment) necessary, we forgive him; and we should teach our children to behave in the same way towards each other. However, if there are jobs to be done about the house, or something to be shared between all, then justice, even if applying the idea of treating unequal things unequally, is the standard of judgment. To make the 'unequal' idea quite clear, our children being different ages, we might ask the eldest, say nine or ten years of age, to go and weed the garden (as long as it's not *too* big!); whereas for the youngest, say three or four years old, to carry a plate of buns to the table without spilling any of them is as much as he can manage.

Moderation

Justice is very much tied up with moderation. In His Tablet to Sulṭán 'Abdu'l-Azíz, Bahá'u'lláh says:

> Overstep not the bounds of moderation, and deal justly with them that serve thee. Bestow upon them according to their needs and not to the extent that will enable them to lay up riches for themselves, to deck their persons, to embellish their homes, to acquire the things that are of no benefit unto them, and to be numbered with the extravagant. Deal with them with undeviating justice, so that none among them may either suffer want, or be pampered with luxuries.[33]

In another passage He says:

> Whoso cleaveth to justice, can, under no circumstances, transgress the limits of moderation. He discerneth the truth in all things, through the guidance of Him Who is the All-Seeing.[34]

These Writings could also be applied in the home.

Moderation can, however, be used as a jolly good excuse for a little quiet self-indulgence. One meets this attitude particularly with drink, of course. 'Moderation in all things!' is the cry. Well, if one believes that it should be in *all* things, how about a little moderate thieving, drug-taking, wife-swapping, black magic, lying and even murder?

Bahá'u'lláh Himself says moderation is desirable; but because He knows human weakness, He makes sure that we are prevented from indulging even moderately in those things which do both ourselves and others harm – by forbidding them.

Self-defence

Justice means fairness to oneself as well as to other people. The Báb set the example in both directions:

> One day the Báb asked that some honey be purchased for Him. The price at which it had been bought seemed to Him exorbitant. He refused it and said: 'Honey of a superior quality could no doubt have been purchased at a lower price. I who am your example have been a merchant by profession. It behoves you in all your transactions to follow in My way. You must neither defraud your neighbour nor allow him to defraud you. Such was the way of your Master. The shrewdest and ablest of men were unable to deceive Him, nor did He on His part choose to act ungenerously towards the meanest and most helpless of creatures.' He insisted that the attendant who had made that purchase should return and bring back to Him a honey superior in quality and cheaper in price.[35]
>
> I often heard those who were closely associated with Him testify to the purity of His character, to the charm of His manners, to His self-effacement, to His high integrity, and to His extreme devotion to God. A certain man confided to His

care a trust, requesting Him to dispose of it at a fixed price. When the Báb sent him the value of that article, the man found that the sum which he had been offered considerably exceeded the limit which he had fixed. He immediately wrote to the Báb, requesting Him to explain the reason. The Báb replied: 'What I have sent you is entirely your due. There is not a single farthing in excess of what is your right. There was a time when the trust you had delivered to Me had attained this value. Failing to sell it at that price, I now feel it My duty to offer you the whole of that sum!' However much the Báb's client entreated Him to receive back the sum in excess, the Báb persisted in refusing.[36]

'Abdu'l-Bahá says we should not be kind to a tyrant,[37] and Bahá'u'lláh, addressing the kings of the earth, says:

> Should any one among you take up arms against another, rise ye all against him, for this is naught but manifest justice.[38]

There must be realism in our attitude to this question where our children are concerned. 'Abdu'l-Bahá says:

> There are some who imagine that an innate sense of human dignity will prevent man from committing evil actions and insure his spiritual and material perfection. That is, that an individual who is characterized with natural intelligence, high resolve, and a driving zeal, will, without any consideration for the severe punishments consequent on evil acts, or for the great rewards of righteousness, instinctively refrain from inflicting harm on his fellow men and will hunger and thirst to do good. And yet, if we ponder the lessons of history it will become evident that this very sense of honor and dignity is itself one of the bounties deriving from the instructions of the Prophets of God. We also observe in infants the signs of aggression and lawlessness, and that if a child is deprived of a teacher's instructions his undesirable qualities increase from one moment to the next. It is therefore clear that the emergence of this natural sense of human dignity and honor is the result of education. Secondly, even if we grant for the sake of the argument that

instinctive intelligence and an innate moral quality would prevent wrongdoing, it is obvious that individuals so characterized are as rare as the philosopher's stone. An assumption of this sort cannot be validated by mere words, it must be supported by the facts. Let us see what power in creation impels the masses toward righteous aims and deeds!

Aside from this, if that rare individual who does exemplify such a faculty should also become an embodiment of the fear of God, it is certain that his strivings toward righteousness would be strongly reinforced.[39]

Shoghi Effendi says:

Regarding your question about children fighting: the statement of the Master, not to strike back, should not be taken so extremely literally that Bahá'í children must accept to be bullied and thrashed. If they can manage to show a better way of settling disputes than by active self-defence, they should naturally do so.[40]

Obedience

This most necessary basic spiritual law depends, I think, on two things: our love for the one requiring us to obey and the reasonableness of the demands.

Babies and small children are little egoists: their soul-consciousness is dormant and has to be awakened by training. They view the world and everything in it with themselves, their needs and desires as the centre of it. There is nothing wrong or abnormal about this. It is part of the instinct for survival which we share with animals. But whereas such a manifestation of this instinct is acceptable in animals, it is not acceptable in humans and has to be restrained, sublimated and redirected.

It is to be hoped that our children love us. Before they are even conscious of the meaning of the word, they should have been nursed, hugged, kissed, taken on the knee and played with, as well as cared for in every other way, so that when they in their turn throw their arms round our necks, kiss us and say, 'I love you!', they have some idea of the emotion they are trying to express. This is the true foundation of obedience and it begins the day they are born.

The reasonableness of the demands is, of course, entirely dependent on the child's age and state of health. In the past, it is a well-documented fact that the demands made upon children were sometimes so excessive it is a wonder that any of them survived. You have only to read social history or some nineteenth-century novelists to be thankful that you yourself, let alone your children, did not live in such child-repressing times.

It is helpful to have read (and preferably studied) at least some good books on elementary psychology in general and child psychology in particular, as a preparation for marriage and family life (Bahá'í psychologists please take the hint and write some!), so that one has some idea what it is reasonable to expect children of various ages to be able to do. For instance, one cannot expect a child of two to be able to sit still, remain silent or concentrate on anything for more than a minute or two, whereas by the time he is eight he should be able to do all these things for much longer periods.

Obedience is also easier to obtain if one does not merely stop at the negative 'Don't!' but diverts the child's attention to something else. It requires that one is always one jump ahead and has a lively imagination; but these are some of the demands on *us* consequent upon making demands on our children. If we see that our child is heading for danger, or is already in it, we should try to remain calm and refrain from passing on our fear to our child at the moment of crisis. I remember vividly my first *conscious* lesson in child psychology, in my early twenties.

I was staying with a friend who had some tall fir trees at the bottom of her garden. One morning she heard a shout, 'Mummy! Look at me!' Through the window she beheld her four-year-old son practically at the top of one of these trees. Her heart must have missed a beat but she stifled her immediate desire to scream at him, thus frightening him and possibly causing an accident. Instead, with supreme self-control and presence of mind, she called out pleasantly, 'Oh, Michael, how terribly clever of you! Now do show me how you get down.' Needless to say, he did. Her object was thus achieved without any trouble at all.

Or there may be occasions when you don't so much want *entirely* to prevent your toddler from doing what he is doing, as to get him to do it in a different way – for instance, how he treats the cat. Small children have no idea that the animal is alive, has feelings and can be hurt. It's just another furry toy with some kind of internal mechanism that enables it to miaow and move about without a key. A tail like that is irresistible. It's specially designed for pulling and pull it he continually will, unless you stop him. Instead of merely shouting, 'Don't *do* that! I tell you, she'll scratch you!' you could try a positive attempt to obey 'Abdu'l-Bahá's instruction that we must teach our children to be kind to animals, and say, mildly, 'Don't hurt pussy. Stroke her gently (doing it yourself and getting the toddler to do it too), ever so gently . . . that's right. Listen, she's purring now. She likes that. But she doesn't like it when you pull her tail, because that hurts. *Gently* now. Stroke her fur *this* way . . .'

Occasionally, a rather aggressive child may be addicted to biting other children and this can be very distressing, not only for the bitten child, who is in pain, but also for the aggressive one's mother, who suffers a different kind of pain. After repeated tellings not to, which have no effect, you may feel that, like the Mikado, you must make the punishment fit the crime. As a family, we once experienced this unfortunate habit. We were at a children's birthday party where none of the children was more than two years of age. Our hostess's little boy was the aggressive one. She warned all the mothers present not to leave him alone in the room with another child, especially our youngest, who was only six or seven months old and was sitting in a high chair. All went well for some time but a moment came when the vigilance was relaxed. We all heard a roar of pain and rushed in to find the baby with a red circle on his cheek, the edges of which showed the evidences of teeth marks. While the baby was being comforted, Aggressive One's mother went in search of him, brought him back into the room, pointed to the crying baby and said to him, 'Now, Christopher, what did I tell you? I told you if you did that once more, I would do it to you, so that you could know what it feels like.' She proceeded to do just that – not in anger and not hard enough to draw blood; but quite hard enough to hurt. Christopher roared in his turn – but he never did it again.

In all these examples obedience was obtained, one immediately, the others later and by different methods. We have to try to use our imagination every time we want to be obeyed and devise all kinds of variations in our efforts to be so. The third example is extreme and it is to be hoped that this sort of thing is necessary only very rarely; but it could be seen as a demonstration of justice – love applied to the group.

As our children gradually learn to love the Master and the Manifestation of God, they will be willing to obey their injunctions, exhortations and laws. When they get old enough to start asking 'Why?', we should be ready with the answers from our own experience and study and from obeying them ourselves. In their Naw-Rúz Message of 1974, the Universal House of Justice says:

The education of children in the teachings of the Faith must be regarded as an essential obligation of every Bahá'í parent . . . It should include moral instruction by word and example and active participation by children in Bahá'í community life.

The implication behind this is that we as parents should be acquainted with the word – that is, the precept – and be able to give a reason for it, as well as ourselves setting the example. We should not imagine, however, that merely because our children love us they will always want to do as we tell them. Far from it! There will be plenty of times when the response to our demand will be pouting, crying, temper and other unpleasantness. To handle this situation successfully, we need to be quite certain, in the first place, that what we are asking is reasonable. We need also to have a vision of the kind of adult we hope ultimately to produce – one who conforms as far as he or she can to the Divine Standard set by the beloved Master – and to keep this vision always in mind. If we will do this, we shall be less likely to make demands on our children that simply reflect our own mood or whim at any particular moment. If we do not want them to say 'No!' or 'I won't!' in response to our instruction, then we must set them the example by pausing to think before immediately saying 'No' ourselves when they say 'Please may I . . . ?' How often does one hear this going on between mothers and children, and how regrettably often does mother give in to persistent pressure! If we say 'No', we should mean it and maintain it; so it is important that it shouldn't be said too often. The child has to learn to obey as well as to do as he wishes. It is important that we, as parents, should be quite clear in our minds where 'No' has to mean 'No' and where we can say, 'Come, now, and let us reason together.'[41] It does, of course, take longer to train children in this way, so it is important that we should not be too occupied with other things which cut down our available time and also our patience. Of all the people we meet, our own children are the most likely to become Bahá'ís and it would be tragic if we were spending so much time 'working for the Faith' that we neglected those who are under our very noses.

It is also important that both father and mother agree on what is to be expected of the children and stick to it, otherwise they will try to play one off against the other in order to get what they want. In cases where one isn't certain, it is as well to ask, 'What does Daddy say?' (or Mummy, as the case may be), and if one's children have been taught to be honest, they will *have* sometimes to admit that the other parent has already said what they fear this one is going to. Unity between father and mother in such matters is essential and guarantees a much smoother passage in the achievement of obedience; added to which it gives a sense of security and knowing where he stands to any child who decides to 'try it on'.

Another aspect of obedience is that the children should learn to submit to the wishes of the majority, where this is applicable. For instance, when the family is on holiday, the parents will decide where to go on any outings they may wish to undertake when the children are small; but the time may come when one of them will say, 'I'd rather go to such-a-place' and before you know where you are a full-scale argument has developed. The best way to overcome this is for the family to decide that each of them in turn will choose a place to visit and the rest will agree to go there, willingly and happily, whether they originally wanted to or not. This arrangement is very good training for accepting majority decisions on a local spiritual assembly at a later date.

Courtesy

In the *Kitáb-i-Aqdas*[42] Bahá'u'lláh tells us to be courteous and there is a passage in the *Gleanings* where we are bidden to let truthfulness and courtesy be our adorning.[43]

If one has been brought up to observe all the niceties of conventional behaviour, with almost everything one does regulated by the minutiae of 'acceptable' manners, one's conscience can become so overburdened with guilt feelings if one puts a little toe, let alone a foot wrong, that to commit a very small error of social etiquette becomes almost as great a sin as telling a lie. Certainly we are exhorted to observe the customs of the country we live in, but as the details of what are considered good manners vary the wide world over we need to think more deeply about this matter.

Courtesy and good manners, it has always seemed to me, should be based on respect for and consideration of other people. I suppose, for instance, if you lived as a hermit in the depths of the countryside, you could shovel your food into your mouth without a care, as there would be nobody there to see (though who knows but that even the rabbits wouldn't stare at you in disgust!) but it is certainly not a pretty sight to watch somebody sitting opposite to you at table behaving in this way.

Again the Golden Rule comes into it; for if we like other people to be courteous and well-mannered towards us, then we should be courteous and well-mannered towards them on the same basis. In the *Lawḥ-i-Dunyá* (Tablet of the World) Bahá'u'lláh says:

> O people of God! I admonish you to observe courtesy. For above all else it is the prince of virtues. Well is it with him who is illumined with the light of courtesy and is attired with the vesture of uprightness. Whoso is endued with courtesy hath indeed attained a sublime station. It is hoped that this Wronged

One and everyone else may be enabled to acquire it, hold fast unto it, observe it, and fix our gaze upon it. This is a binding command which hath streamed forth from the Pen of the Most Great Name.[44]

Three things are particularly noteworthy in this passage: courtesy is called the 'prince of virtues'; the courteous person has attained a 'sublime station'; and it is a 'binding command'. We therefore need to instruct our children in courtesy and good manners from a very young age. Perhaps the very first lesson they learn in courtesy is to say 'Please' and 'Thank you' before and after being handed what they want.

If we base our training on respect for and consideration of others, we shall find that we can manage quite happily wherever we may be. Courteous, well-mannered people are pleasant to be with whatever country they come from, because respect for and consideration of others are universal virtues. It is true that, if we travel a lot or mix with those of different nationalities from ourselves, it helps to be aware of certain areas where codes are not quite the same as our own – or words have assumed a different meaning – in order not to commit the occasional embarrassing *faux pas*; but in general, a courteous, well-mannered person in one country is a courteous, well-mannered person in any country.

It is also true that courtesy oils the wheels of society and helps it to function with the minimum of friction. How pleasant it is to have dealings with a courteous shop-assistant, bus conductor, foreman, etc.; and no doubt it is equally pleasant for them to have dealings with courteous customers, travellers or workmen.

If we wish our children to be courteous and well-mannered towards us, then it goes without saying that we must not think that, because they are 'only our children', we are exempted from the need to set the example. So, 'Go and get my hammer from the kitchen drawer' becomes, 'Would you be kind enough to fetch my hammer from the kitchen drawer? . . . Thank you', or 'Pass me that book' becomes 'Please will you pass me that book? . . . Thanks'; and if we expect our children, when they are old enough to go out without us, to tell us where they are going, do we return the compliment, even if it's only to do the shopping?

Kindness

Kindness does not have to be confused with indulgence, for in the end this is not kindness but a form of cruelty. Bahá'u'lláh enjoins kindness to animals, 'how much more unto his fellow-man, him who is endowed with the power of utterance'.[45] In connection with animals, the children must be taught to have what Albert Schweitzer calls 'reverence for life'* and never to torment or hurt one of God's creatures (killing ferocious animals is excepted but I do not wish to go into this here).

There really is not any need to discuss the question of kindness in any detail. All that needs to be emphasised, perhaps, is that kindness is something which should always be extended to each other by all members of the family, without cessation and without stint. There is a story from China about an old man called Chang Kung whose children, grandchildren and great-grandchildren all lived together in a large compound after the manner of those days. The old man grew happier and happier as his family increased and it was said that he also loved animals so much that at one time there were a hundred dogs living in the compound too. The family became famous far and

---

* See the relevant chapters in *My Life and Thought* and *Civilisation and Ethics* by Albert Schweitzer.

wide but not on account of its size. It was because they never quarrelled, any of them, not even the children. In time the Emperor came to hear of it and decided to visit Chang Kung to discover the secret of the harmony of this remarkable family. Chang Kung called for a bamboo tablet, his brush and ink. He wrote and wrote until he had filled the tablet, and when he had finished he placed it in the Emperor's hands. The Emperor was amazed to find that, although he had written such a lot, there was only one word on the tablet. 'Yes,' replied the old man, 'but that is the golden secret: KINDNESS – over and over again.'

Self-discipline

Self-discipline is another quality which children have to learn. There are many areas of their lives where it is necessary: controlling their bodily appetites, keeping themselves clean, doing their homework or practising their music, not giving way to temper, saying their prayers and so on. Self-discipline is intimately tied up with the acquisition of good habits and good habits are only acquired after a lengthy period of doing the same thing day after day. To be able to discipline *oneself* has behind it perhaps years of being expected to do or not do certain things until they become so automatic that one doesn't even think about them.

Self-discipline is also a great asset in times of trouble. If one has certain things firmly embedded in one's mind and behaviour when life is running smoothly, then this comes to one's aid when there is a crisis in one's life. One can cope with the crisis because the good habits and self-discipline of one's ordinary life can look after themselves.

The opposite of self-discipline is self-indulgence. The one who indulges his greed will eventually make himself ill; the one who doesn't wash will find that people avoid him; the one who will not do his homework or practising will make no progress; the one who cannot control his temper will lose his friends; the one who neglects his prayers will suffer increasing remoteness from God.

Of course, the acquiring of good habits and self-discipline by our children implies the instilling of them on the part of the parents and in the early years it usually falls to mothers to do this. The patient pegging away at this training can sometimes be exasperating and it often requires much self-discipline on our part not to shout at them when they have once more forgotten to wash behind the ears or make their beds. What an optimistic mother it was who once said to me, 'I've told her four times already this morning and still she doesn't remember. I should have thought four times was enough.' No, dear mother, it is not. We have to be prepared to tell our children the same thing ten, twenty, or even fifty times a day, if necessary, in order to inculcate that habit. Even then, we shall probably find they are still leaving doors open when they are twenty and – shall it be told? – Yes! – some even when they are thirty . . .

Society is disintegrating fast and it becomes ever more necessary to instil into our children the need to acquire the virtues of Bahá'í life. The minute they go to school they are thrown into the lion's den. We must help them to be like Daniel, and be so true to God's Faith that the lions are unable to tear them to pieces.

Parents stand as God

When our children are very small, we their parents stand as God to them, but eventually we must help them to transfer their love for us and their belief in our infallibility and omnipotence to God Himself. Growing up is partly a process of learning – sometimes painfully – that one's parents are not infallible or sinless and may sometimes let one down; but one can learn that God never does, nor does the Blessed Perfection. We are fortunate in having the person of 'Abdu'l-Bahá for children to relate to first, because they can understand Him better than the Manifestation of God and certainly better than God Himself. 'Abdu'l-Bahá is unique in religious history. It is as though God has accepted man's need to have someone understandable and approachable to relate to and has provided such a one in the person of 'Abdu'l-Bahá. He is quite separate from the Godhead. Indeed, He is quite separate from the Manifestation of God. So while He satisfies this need, there can never be any confusion of doctrine. That we use capital letters when referring to Him is a sign of our reverence for His station – so far above ours – and does not imply that we are muddled in our thinking.

We parents can help in the process of change-over by explaining to our children that we *are* sometimes wrong and *do* make mistakes – and apologising for them when we do. Far from losing authority over them, or whatever other fear is at the back of our minds when we refuse to admit we are mistaken, our children will respect us more. *They know*, and are not taken in by the Daddy-is-always-right mentality or the Mummy-doeth-whatsoever-she-willeth attitude. In this way we can gradually wean them from total dependence on us as their parents and help them to transfer their allegiance to God. Each one of us has to make our own relationship with God; each one of us has to try to live the Bahá'í life in our own way and each one of us has to try to understand the Writings for ourselves. Our ultimate aim as parents should surely be to help our children to do this.

Rear children to be staunch in faith

A most important aim for us as parents should be to rear our children to be staunch in faith. Bahá'u'lláh says:

> ... a child who removeth himself from the religion of God will not act in such a way as to win the good pleasure of his parents and his Lord. For every praiseworthy deed is born out of the light of religion, and lacking this supreme bestowal the child will not turn away from any evil, nor will he draw nigh unto any good.[46]

> Man is even as steel, the essence of which is hidden: through admonition and explanation, good counsel and education, that essence will be brought to light. If, however, he be allowed to remain in his original condition, the corrosion of lusts and appetites will effectively destroy him.[47]

'Abdu'l-Bahá tells us that if we train our children properly 'they will remain safe from every test'.[48] This doesn't mean that they won't have tests, but that they will overcome them. He says:

> In a time to come, morals will degenerate to an extreme degree. It is essential that children be reared in the Bahá'í way, that they may find happiness both in this world and the next. If not, they shall be beset by sorrows and troubles, for human happiness is founded upon spiritual behaviour.[49]

This time is already upon us. Each day brings news of this degeneration more shocking than the last – and things will no doubt get a lot worse yet.

If we are staunch ourselves, we are more likely to produce this quality in our children. 'Religion is caught, not taught', they say, and deep down this is true. How much our faith means to *us* will soon be understood by our children:

> Know that in every home where God is praised and prayed

to, and His kingdom proclaimed, that home is a garden of God and a paradise of His happiness.[50]

Serving the Cause should be put at the forefront of our thinking and at the centre of our life. We must show our children *by our actions* that we believe in Bahá'u'lláh with the very essence of our being and that we believe teaching the Cause to be 'the most meritorious of all deeds'.[51] Perhaps the highest achievement which we can aim at in this direction is to create in our children the desire to pioneer.

We should teach our children to *strive*: to accept challenge in life. Too often these days one feels that this excellent attribute of striving is neglected; but children – and most grown-ups for that matter – respond to a challenge. A challenge isn't an impossibility. It is something which you may think is difficult but not utterly beyond you if you exert yourself. 'He will never deal unjustly with anyone,' Bahá'u'lláh tells us, 'neither will He task a soul beyond its power.'[52] Increase in this power of the soul is the reason for all tests. At the same time we should encourage our children to feel that they *can* overcome the difficulty; that it should be looked upon as a challenge which they can meet and that with God's help they will win through; it should not be seen as a problem to be used as an excuse for not doing something. In the little book called *A Bahá'í Child's A.B.C.** this idea is conveyed under the letter 'V for Victory'.

Hardship

'Abdu'l-Bahá gives a vision of the future which is very inspiring and then tells us what we should do about helping to achieve it:

---

* Wilmette: Bahá'í Publishing Trust 1944.

Wherefore, O loved ones of God! Make ye a mighty effort till you yourselves betoken this advancement and all these confirmations, and become focal centres of God's blessings, daysprings of the light of His unity, promoters of the gifts and graces of civilized life. Be ye in that land vanguards of the perfections of humankind; carry forward the various branches of knowledge, be active and progressive in the field of inventions and the arts. Endeavour to rectify the conduct of men, and seek to excel the whole world in moral character. While the children are yet in their infancy feed them from the breast of heavenly grace, foster them in the cradle of all excellence, rear them in the embrace of bounty. Give them the advantage of every useful kind of knowledge. Let them share in every new and rare and wondrous craft and art. Bring them up to work and strive, and accustom them to hardship. Teach them to dedicate their lives to matters of great import, and inspire them to undertake studies that will benefit mankind.[53]

Note particularly the sentence, 'Bring them up to work and strive and accustom them to hardship.'* So much modern thought moves in the opposite direction: you must never be unhappy, you must never be uncomfortable, you must never be allowed to suffer in any way! The result of this will be a race of jelly-fish: flabby-muscled, flabby-minded, flabby-willed and flabby-spirited. Hard work and hardship never hurt anyone, least of all when undertaken in the course of a life dedicated to matters of great import. Indeed, it does us good.

However, having said this, it might be as well to offer some suggestions as to what could be interpreted as 'hardship'. Obviously we are not proposing a return to sending small children down coal mines or up chimneys; we don't mean by this that children should be regularly whipped, fed on bread and water for a week, or turned out into the snow without shoes and only thin rags on their

---

* This word can also be translated 'lack of ease'.

backs. Though heaven knows, in some parts of the world even today, some children's existence is no better than this – and in some cases, worse. This will, in time, surely be put right; but the question of what is meant by hardship will always remain.

Hardship must always be a relative condition, for what is hardship for one child, even in the same family, is not necessarily so for another. It isn't exactly paradise, at seven or eight years old, to be required to sit down two days after Christmas and make a start on writing 'thank you letters' for presents, which must be done at the rate of three a day until they are finished. Some children take to it more easily than others, depending on their inclinations and abilities. Some, good at English, will write interesting letters and have the three finished fairly quickly, while others, to whom composition is a burden, will get as far as writing the address and 'Dear Uncle —— and Aunty ——' and then sit gazing into space for the next half-hour wondering what to say.

Other examples of what children in the modern world might feel as hardship include being given only a small sum each week as pocket money and of that, being expected to put some into the children's Fund box and some into their respective savings boxes, leaving very little to spend (and then being encouraged not to fritter it away but wait until it has accumulated and will buy something worth having), when all the other children in their class have a great deal more and can spend it all on themselves if they want to; or not being allowed sweets except, say, at the end of lunch on Saturdays and Sundays, followed by the statutory piece of apple to clean the teeth, because their parents have ideas about healthy eating habits; or having their television viewing strictly controlled by the parents and otherwise not being allowed to touch it. To us, examples such as these may seem nothing much and part of normal character training, but to the children they may well be seen as hardship and if they question why they should be subjected to these strictures, we should be ready to explain our reasons for enforcing them.

If the hardship is undertaken in order to help others, this is even better. In some instances it gives them a sympathetic understanding of world problems as well. Some Quaker meetings (i.e. the local group) hold monthly 'hunger lunches'; you are given a slice of wholemeal bread and butter and a small piece of cheese to eat and a cup of tea or coffee to drink. You put into the collecting box for Oxfam (or whatever it is) the full price you would have paid for a meal in a café. To children of ten or twelve, especially boys, who can easily consume two large helpings of both courses provided for their dinner at home, this abstemiousness is quite hard; even more so if it is followed by a double school period of rugby or football. However, if our children are happy, encouraged in their school work and practising, and given plenty to occupy their lively minds in the shape of hobbies, 'outside interests', family outings or doing things together as a family at home and so on, they are much less likely to feel hardship in these directions because they will be given so very much more in others.

The most important thing they have, which other children do not, is the Faith. Not only the Faith itself, but the fact that their horizons are being continually widened by meeting and mingling with people from all over the world, at Summer Schools, weekend schools and all the usual meetings we take them to, and also having people of other nations and races staying in their homes and visiting them in theirs. I remember saying something to this effect to an Anglican friend many years ago. She replied, 'Your children are very fortunate.' Our children may not see it this way at the time; but when they have grown up they will realise that they were indeed the fortunate ones and that it was all the others who suffered hardship!

So it has become quite clear, from what has been said so far, that character training is far more important than any amount of book-learning; though obviously, it is better to have a good character *and* knowledge and wisdom. 'Abdu'l-Bahá says:

> Training in morals and good conduct is far more important than book learning. A child that is cleanly, agreeable, of good character, well-behaved – even though he be ignorant – is preferable to a child that is rude, unwashed, ill-natured, and yet becoming deeply versed in all the sciences and arts. The reason for this is that the child who conducts himself well, even though he be ignorant, is of benefit to others, while an ill-natured, ill-behaved child is corrupted and harmful to others, even though he be learned. If, however, the child be trained to be both learned and good, the result is light upon light.[54]

4

Family Life

The final sentence of the last quotation in the previous chapter covers both the formal aspect of our children's education and also the informal – what goes on in the home. In so far as this book deals with education in the family setting, we naturally concentrate on this rather than saying much about schooling. We have already learned that the father is to be responsible for his children's scholastic education. It is to the mother's rôle in the family that we must now give some thought.

The mother's rôle

The mother's rôle is supremely important in the upbringing of the children, especially during their early years. We know that the mother is the first teacher of the child: what an inestimable privilege we mothers have – and what a responsibility! Education starts before the baby is born. I believe it is possible to give the child in your womb a spiritual, loving, happy atmosphere in which to develop, by the state of mind you yourself are in during your pregnancy. Once your child is born, education begins in earnest and from his earliest years he should be immersed in the ocean of the Word. 'Abdu'l-Bahá says:

From the very beginning, the children must receive divine education and must continually be reminded to remember their God. Let the love of God pervade their inmost being, commingled with their mother's milk.[1]

It is a well-known fact that, at bedtime, children are receptive. The Master says:

> When the children are ready for bed, let the mother read or sing them the Odes of the Blessed Beauty, so that from their earliest years they will be educated by these verses of guidance.[2]

Bahá'u'lláh is quite explicit on the matter:

> Teach your children what hath been revealed through the Pen of Glory. Instruct them in what hath descended from the heaven of greatness and power. Let them memorize the Tablets of the Merciful . . .[3]

It is perfectly possible for quite young children to understand selected simple passages from any of the Scriptures. If we parents know our *Gleanings*, for example, we can choose sentences and paragraphs suited to our children's understanding at any age, and it is good for them to become acquainted with these volumes from the beginning. They do not need to have everything reduced to words of one syllable if we will take the trouble to explain meanings. If we don't know them ourselves, we can look them up in the dictionary and thus improve our education. Bahá'u'lláh's injunction that we must first teach our own selves can be applied even at this level!

Our aim should be for the children to feel a great love for God, for Bahá'u'lláh and for 'Abdu'l-Bahá and to make their own, very warm, relationship with Them. Let them have a portrait of 'Abdu'l-Bahá in their bedrooms: needless to say, the love of God comes first of all, but with their literal minds it is perhaps easier for them to learn to love someone first with whose face they are familiar. I know of one mother of twins who had a photograph of 'Abdu'l-Bahá on her dressing-table. Her little twins, aged about two, were familiar with this picture and knew Who it was. One day, they came in to see her while she was ill in bed; and passing the picture, one said, 'Uncle Ba!' and the other, not to be outdone in knowledge, added, 'Ha-Ha there!' I'm sure the beloved Master would have loved to be called by such affectionate terminology!

A rich and happy home life should be a joint creation but it is clear from what the Master says that the main responsibility for this, at least in the early years, falls on the mother. There are many ways in which she can achieve it, and it is now that the vital necessity of a good education becomes apparent. If she is well educated, she will have deep joy in passing on to her children her knowledge and abilities and her own special interests; she will take great pride in watching their gifts appear and will do all she can to encourage their development; she will read to them, sing to them, play with them, introducing them gradually to all the wealth of the world's literary, musical and artistic heritage; she will help them to love and appreciate beautiful things, whether created by God in nature or by man in his various creative skills; she will widen their horizons by putting before them the means to learn something of the history and geography of the earth, by means of books, exhibitions, museum visits and so on; she will try to stimulate them to be observant of the world about them and to think for themselves; for these things are not just the responsibility of the schools. She will be there to mend their clothes and attend to their cuts and bruises, to hear them say their vocabulary and to take an interest in their interests; to comfort them when they are sad or hurt and to be a wise and loving counsellor when they quarrel; and all this on top of preparing meals, cleaning the house, doing the washing and ironing and all the other multitude of tasks that are involved in creating a home as distinct from merely running a house.

If the mother will do this – which amounts to helping her children to enjoy life and have enquiring minds – she will find their spiritual education and character training much easier. A child who is happy and has plenty to occupy him is more likely to be good than one who is constantly left to his own devices. A room full of toys and the television on all the time are no substitute for his mother's time and attention.

Bearing in mind all that has been said, there is the controversial question of whether or not young mothers should go out to work when circumstances do not force them to do so; and if they do, at what stage in their children's development they can do so without detriment to family life. Bahá'u'lláh says:

> It is enjoined upon every one of you to engage in some form of occupation, such as crafts, trades and the like.[4]

As He does not specifically address this to men only, women may feel that it applies to them also. Perhaps it does! Certain extracts from the compilations *Family Life* and *Women* would seem to indicate that this is so; but I understand that the Arabic text in the *Kitáb-i-Aqdas* where Bahá'u'lláh requires everyone to work implies useful activity and not necessarily a paid job.*

Three extracts from letters of the Universal House of Justice throw some light on this matter:

> You ask about the admonition that everyone must work, and want to know if this means that you, a wife and mother, must work for a livelihood as your husband does. We are requested to enclose for your perusal an excerpt, 'The twelfth Glad-Tidings',

---

* See article 'Bahá'í Laws on the Status of Men' by Linda and John Walbridge, *World Order* magazine, Fall 1984/Winter 1984–5, p. 26.

from Bahá'u'lláh's 'Tablet of Bis͟hárát'. You will see that the directive is for the friends to be engaged in an occupation which will be of benefit to mankind. Homemaking is a highly honourable and responsible work of fundamental importance for mankind.[5]

The great importance attached to the mother's role derives from the fact that she is the *first* educator of the child. Her attitude, her prayers, even what she eats and her physical condition have a great influence on the child when it is still in the womb. When the child is born, it is she who has been endowed by God with the milk which is the first food designed for it, and it is intended that, if possible, she should be with the baby to train and nurture it in its earliest days and months. This does not mean that the father does not also love, pray for, and care for his baby, but as he has the primary responsibility of providing for the family, his time to be with his child is usually limited, while the mother is usually closely associated with the baby during this intensely formative time when it is growing and developing faster than it ever will again during the whole of its life. As the child grows older and more independent, the relative nature of its relationship with its mother and father modifies and the father can play a greater role.[6]

With regard to your question whether mothers should work outside the home, it is helpful to consider the matter from the perspective of the concept of a Bahá'í family. This concept is based on the principle that the man has primary responsibility for the financial support of the family, and the woman is the chief and primary educator of the children. This by no means implies that these functions are inflexibly fixed and cannot be changed and adjusted to suit particular family situations, nor does it mean that the place of the woman is confined to the home. Rather, while primary responsibility is assigned, it is anticipated that fathers would play a significant role in the education of the children and women could also be breadwinners. As you rightly indicated, 'Abdu'l-Bahá encouraged women to 'participate fully and equally in the affairs of the world'.

In relation to your specific queries, the decision concerning the amount of time a mother may spend in working outside the home depends on circumstances existing within the home, which may vary from time to time. Family consultation will help to provide the answers.[7]

However, we must remember that Bahá'u'lláh's instructions will only be fully understood in a Bahá'í world, where parental, social and industrial relationships will be properly adjusted. It could be, for instance, that eventually the working day will be reduced to four hours. If this should happen, the father and mother could both have a part-time job and there would always be one parent at home. There would be many advantages in this arrangement, not the least of which would be the abolition of 'latch-key children' and a consequent reduction in juvenile delinquency. The indications are that continuing demands for shorter working hours are moving in this direction. The question then arises as to what people are to do with their spare time. As far as parents are concerned, such an arrangement would give them the opportunity to create a rich family life – and this does not imply simply a life contained within the four walls of the house.

Another possibility would be that the Bahá'í community in any given place would interact like the members of a family and difficulties in child-minding would be overcome in this way. In days gone by, when many people did not move outside the confines of their town or village, it was common for the 'wider family' – grandparents, uncles, aunts and cousins – to live in close proximity to each other and the children would therefore have other 'homes' to go to if their parents were both, say, working in a mill. They thus had that fundamental feeling of security which is vital for a child's healthy emotional development. In a Bahá'í world, where the members of any particular family would be likely to be scattered over the face of the globe, the local community would, I am sure, act as the 'wider family' in this respect.

However, we have a long way to go before this happens, if it ever does; and even in an ideal society, the fact that it is the mothers who must carry, bear and nurse the children can never be ignored. Any adjustments to the workings of society would have to take this fact into account, perhaps even pay mothers an allowance for several years to stay at home and look after their family, treating it as a very important job which should be a paid one like any other.

In the meantime, we have to live in society as it is constituted today and this can – and often does – present problems. 'Abdu'l-Bahá says:

> O maid-servants of the Merciful! It is incumbent upon you to train the children from their earliest babyhood! It is incumbent upon you to beautify their morals! It is incumbent upon you to attend to them under all aspects and circumstances, inasmuch as God – glorified and exalted is He! – hath ordained mothers to be the primary trainers of children and infants. This is a great and important affair and a high and exalted position, and it is not allowable to slacken therein at all!
>
> If thou walkest in this right path, thou wouldst become a real mother to the children, both spiritually and materially.[8]

'Abdu'l-Bahá no doubt knew that the emancipation of women would bring with it problems of dissatisfaction with their traditional rôle, and wrote strongly about mothers in consequence. His Writings on the place of women in society are very challenging and give much food for thought; but I think perhaps His exhortations to mothers are an attempt to adjust the balance which He foresaw would become overweighted with wrong conceptions about what women's emancipation implied:

Wherefore, O ye loving mothers, know ye that in God's sight, the best of all ways to worship Him is to educate the children and train them in all the perfections of humankind; and no nobler deed than this can be imagined . . .[9]

My personal feeling is that, at present, this country (and I do not have experience of any other to give me the right to express an opinion about it) does not appreciate and therefore does not encourage the creation of such a rich and stimulating family life as we have been talking about. Our educational system, with its over-emphasis on intellectual attainment, has a lot to answer for in this respect. There is usually quite inadequate training given in domestic science and economy and virtually none in looking after children and caring for their needs. Once upon a time, when families were large and mother was perforce there all the time, this training took place in the home without the girls being aware, almost, of what was going on. Nowadays, when families are reduced to two or three and mother is out at work a lot of the time, home-making has to be taught rather than merely absorbed. If it is right that schools should teach children how babies arrive in the world in the first place, it would seem logical that they should also give instruction in looking after them once they have arrived. Owing, I think, to historical factors which have left a legacy of negative attitudes to domestic chores, 'a woman's place is in the home' and so on, many girls may feel that home life is nothing more than washing nappies and scrubbing the kitchen floor. Unless one enjoys it, domestic work *is* boring; but so is tending a machine for eight hours a day five days a week. There are boring elements in any job: why should we mothers wish ours to be the exception?

I am not suggesting that mothers should be tied to the kitchen sink all the time. God forbid! There must be many women – myself included – who are not completely satisfied by domestic chores and want something more to occupy their minds and their time. A woman who has embarked on a career before she was married, such as medicine or some other profession requiring a long training, may feel she does not want to waste this training, either for her own satisfaction or for the service she can render to other people, when she has a family. I am not concerned with the rights and wrongs of the matter – it is a controversial issue, as has already been said. Every couple must decide for themselves what they are going to do. What I *am* concerned about is that we should all think deeply about what we mean by 'family life' and our part as mothers within it; and before we decide to return to work we try to ensure that the quality of our family life will not suffer as a consequence. As husbands and fathers will be profoundly affected by the consequences of a wife and mother who is doing even a part-time, let alone a full-time job, the decision about returning to work after the arrival of the first child, or any subsequent children, should be a joint one. The idea that one isn't working if one stays at home is a reflection of the historical legacy referred to above. My reply to anyone who asked me if I worked has always been, 'Yes, very hard – but not for gain!'

It would take too long to discuss the matter fully; the mother's rôle is a vast subject and there is no room to go into it in any detail here. It could well form the basis for study classes and weekend or day schools. As the Master says, it is a great and important affair, and if we want our children to grow up into steadfast, loving Bahá'ís, we should give a great deal of attention to it.

Prayer

Prayer for the child should begin the minute he is

conceived. When he is born and until he is old enough to speak, you can say prayers aloud over his cot night and morning and this will give him a wonderful feeling of security and peace, especially at night. Once he can speak, he should be taught to repeat the simple prayers, half a sentence at a time. Never mind if he doesn't understand them – neither do we, fully! Children should never remember a time when they were not familiar with the prayers; there are now several publications of children's prayers, so the task is easy.

A word might perhaps be said at this point about our attitude to prayer. The Universal House of Justice wishes to see 'standards of decency, dignity and reverence' become 'deeply implanted in Bahá'í consciousness'.[10] Nowhere is reverence more markedly demonstrated than in the physical posture we adopt when praying – it reveals more than anything else how we view our relationship to God. Reverence for God – and therefore life – stems from a deep and devoted love for Him. If we have this, we shall not go far wrong. The more we can develop this love, the more unworthy of it we shall feel ourselves to be; and the more we feel *this*, the more we shall feel that the only proper place for us, in our relationship to God, is as low as we can get, flat on our faces on the floor. In the West we do not by habit prostrate ourselves in prayer; but with increasing awareness, it may begin to seem irreverent to pray lounging in a chair with our legs crossed.* There is an old mediaeval carol which contains a picturesque phrase: 'The knees of my hert sall I bow',† and while it is true that what you feel inside is what matters, I personally believe that we shall help our children to develop a right relationship to God if they see us adopt reverent postures

---

* See 'The Dynamic Force of Example', p. 91 (Bahá'í Comprehensive Deepening Programme, American Bahá'í Publishing Trust, 1974).
† These are not spelling mistakes, but mediaeval English!

while praying. If we have taught them to be reverent during their prayers at home and required of them that they should be quiet and give their whole minds to what they are doing, they will be better prepared to sit reverently and quietly on their chairs when they are in meetings; but it goes without saying that *we* have got to set the example.

Discipline

Although much emphasis is placed by the Master on a loving home, discipline is also needed. He says:

> Let them strive by day and by night to establish within their children faith and certitude, the fear of God, the love of the Beloved of the worlds, and all good qualities and traits. Whensoever a mother seeth that her child hath done well, let her praise and applaud him and cheer his heart; and if the slightest undesirable trait should manifest itself, let her counsel the child and punish him, and use means based on reason, even a slight verbal chastisement should this be necessary. It is not, however, permissible to strike a child, or vilify him, for the child's character will be totally perverted if he be subjected to blows or verbal abuse.[11]

Some thoughts about the last sentence of this paragraph might be helpful. It should be considered in the light of the Guardian's advice to an individual believer:

> Discipline of some sort, whether physical, moral or intellectual, is indeed indispensable, and no training can be said to be complete and fruitful if it disregards this element.[12]

The fact that Shoghi Effendi includes physical discipline as a necessary element, along with moral and intellectual, implies that he did not rule it out. There is a world of difference between the occasional smack, given only after repeated verbal warnings have been ignored or when no more effective form of discipline pertains, and the constant resort to immediate and continual violence which is implied in the words 'subjected to blows'. The important thing is that any physical chastisement which is given should be administered mildly and in love, not in anger – for this is to relieve the feelings of the parent rather than to do any good to the child. Much more could be discussed on this subject and parents must use their discretion in the matter. In passing, it is worthy of note that on one occasion Bahá'u'lláh Himself saw fit to administer corporal punishment to His son Muḥammad-'Alí. Admittedly, Muḥammad-'Alí was grown up and richly deserved his punishment, but this doesn't alter the fact that his Father felt it necessary 'with His own hand' to chastise one of His own children.[13]

Family rights

In the days when I was a young mother there was a lot of talk about never letting children be unhappy. You should never say 'Mummy's tired' as a reason for not wanting to respond to a request to expend energy, because they wouldn't understand what you meant. You should never get cross with them because you might do them irreparable psychological harm. I remember the delight with which I read a newspaper article called 'Anger in the Home', by a doctor who had a bit more sense. His point was that if you showed anger occasionally, it gave the children the idea that you *had* some standards, and there *were* things you cared about and limits beyond which you could not permit them to go without showing your feelings. Probably the same doctor pointed out that if you always tried to behave like an automatons the children would never learn to consider you. As usual, 'Abdu'l-Bahá gives us the right attitude:

According to the teachings of Bahá'u'lláh the family, being a human unit, must be educated according to the rules of sanctity. All the virtues must be taught the family. The integrity of the family bond must be constantly considered, and the rights of the individual members must not be transgressed. The rights of the son, the father, the mother – none of them must be transgressed; none of them must be arbitrary. Just as the son has certain obligations to his father, the father, likewise, has certain obligations to his son. The mother, the sister and other members of the household have their certain prerogatives. All these rights and prerogatives must be conserved, yet the unity of the family must be sustained. The injury of one shall be considered the injury of all; the comfort of each, the comfort of all; the honor of one, the honor of all.[14]

But the question of family rights is not a one-sided affair:

There are also certain sacred duties on children toward parents, which duties are written in the Book of God, as belonging to God.* The (children's) prosperity in this world and the Kingdom depends upon the good pleasure of parents, and without this they will be in manifest loss.[15]

In one of His Tablets 'Abdu'l-Bahá makes the filial relationship clear:

O dear one of 'Abdu'l-Bahá! Be the son of thy father and be the fruit of that tree. Be a son that hath been born of his soul and heart and not only of the water and clay. A real son is such an one as hath branched from the spiritual part of a man. I ask God that thou mayest be at all times confirmed and strengthened.[16]

The crossroads

There is a point in a young child's development where one

---

* In 'Questions and Answers', an appendix to the *Kitáb-i-Aqdas*, Bahá'u'lláh lays upon children the obligation of serving their parents and categorically states that after the recognition of the oneness of God, the most important of all duties for children is to have due regard for the rights of their parents. (Footnote in explanation of the above quotation, given in *Bahá'í Education*, p. 54.)

can see all the potential needed to become delinquent. He shows traits which, if not trained in the right way, can easily lead to problems. One might call this point the crossroads, because it is now that it is *essential* that we strain every nerve to train our children – and sometimes it *is* a strain. Again, we will apply to the home instructions which were intended for schools, because if the home does not insist on the same standards as the school, the latter will be virtually fighting a losing battle:

> The more cleanly the pupils are, the better; they should be immaculate. The school must be located in a place where the air is delicate and pure. The children must be carefully trained to be most courteous and well-behaved. They must be constantly encouraged and made eager to gain all the summits of human accomplishment, so that from their earliest years they will be taught to have high aims, to conduct themselves well, to be chaste, pure, and undefiled, and will learn to be of powerful resolve and firm of purpose in all things. Let them not jest and trifle, but earnestly advance unto their goals, so that in every situation they will be found resolute and firm . . .
>
> Children are even as a branch that is fresh and green; they will grow up in whatever way you train them.[17]

In other words, the acquisition of good habits, rather than letting them grow up to be dirty and untidy, rude, lazy, inconsiderate, undisciplined and weak-willed.

Correction of faults

The Master tells us that 'In creation there is no evil'.[18] It is, of course, sometimes difficult for us, human as we are, to react as we would like in the heat of the moment when our children irritate us; but if we can remember that 'certain qualities and natures innate in some men and apparently blameworthy are not so in reality',[19] we may do better. The Master goes on to explain that,

For example, from the beginning of his life you can see in a nursing child the signs of greed, of anger and of temper. Then, it may be said, good and evil are innate in the reality of man, and this is contrary to the pure goodness of nature and creation. The answer to this is that greed, which is to ask for something more, is a praiseworthy quality provided that it is used suitably. So if a man is greedy to acquire science and knowledge, or to become compassionate, generous and just, it is most praiseworthy. If he exercises his anger and wrath against the bloodthirsty tyrants who are like ferocious beasts, it is very praiseworthy; but if he does not use these qualities in a right way, they are blameworthy.[20]

He also says,

The child must not be oppressed or censured because it is undeveloped; it must be patiently trained.[21]

and again,

If a pupil is told that his intelligence is less than his fellow-pupils, it is a very great drawback and handicap to his progress. He must be encouraged to advance . . .[22]

If this is true in a school, how much more in the home, where comparing one of your children unfavourably with another can result in real emotional disturbance. It may well be the case that one is brighter than another, or better behaved or more sociable and so on. It is not our task as parents to produce uniformity. 'Abdu'l-Bahá says:

Man is not intended to see through the eyes of another, hear through another's ears nor comprehend with another's brain. Each human creature has individual endowment, power and responsibility in the creative plan of God.[23]

If the educational system through which our children must pass doesn't discover these things, then it is even more important for us as parents to find, encourage and train the gifts of all our children, however brilliant or ordinary they may be.

We should also realise that, just as our children inherit our looks and our gifts, they also inherit our temperaments and our faults. It is often our own faults coming out in our children which cause us the greatest aggravation and can be the hardest to cope with; but just as this may be true when they are little, it can also gradually be turned into a bond of understanding as each one – child and parent – tries to control and overcome the fault in him- or herself. Each can thus help the other in a very valuable way. Parents who learn nothing from their children are blind indeed!

Appreciation of differences

The teachings of our Faith help our children to appreciate differences in other people. They also have to meet this head on in the family itself. The first thing that all children have to come to terms with, unless they are 'onlies', is their place in the age order. Being either the older or the younger, or the one in the middle if there are three, has its own special problems for the child concerned. 'Only children' and twins have different problems. However sensitive we think we are being to the emotional needs of each, we can still quite unconsciously put ideas into their heads which may cause them a little worry or distress. One lovely family I know, where both parents are wonderful Bahá'ís and devoted to their children, illustrates this point. There were five children in the family, three boys and two girls, in that order. Because of the age difference between the two older boys and the middle one and the middle one and the little girls, the parents got into the habit of referring to their family as 'the boys and the younger ones'. This was later changed to 'the little ones, the boys and Bobby' (not his real name), Bobby being the one in the middle. One day, hearing this description yet once more, he innocently enquired, 'Aren't *I* a boy?' Poor Bobby! He knew he wasn't a girl, so if he wasn't a boy either, what was he? Perhaps he was an angel. They are supposed to be sexless!

Even size can be a difficulty. Young Gordon (again, not his real name), changing schools at eleven plus, was put into long trousers because he was already almost as big as his brother two years older. '*I* had to wear shorts when *I* started!' came the cry. The answer that young Gordon now looked absolutely terrible in shorts because he had grown so much was not entirely convincing; but age and size are things the children have no control over and they have no alternative but to accept them as facts of life. They had no say in the order in which they arrived, nor have they any in the rate at which they grow; but we can make their passage a little easier, perhaps, by explaining this to them.

Their sex and their temperament will also play their part. Girls' interests have been considered, traditionally, to be different from those of boys. No doubt in general this is true, but we should guard against directing our children into stylised rôles ourselves, by always giving them the kinds of toy they are 'supposed' to want to have. Why *shouldn't* a boy play with dolls if he wants to? Girls are presumed to have a mother instinct; cannot a boy have a father instinct? Why *shouldn't* a girl be given a train set if she wants one? She might be going to turn into a mechanical genius!

Temperament is often a major cause of friction. If one of the children is quick, highly strung and volatile and the other slow and dreamy, there may well be sparks when these temperaments cross each other. The one may be impatient and the other stubborn and you are left with the question, 'When the irresistible force meets the immovable object, what happens?' More than likely a scuffle and you may have to intervene to restore the peace; and you may have to wait until they are grown up before they begin to appreciate each other. As we said at the beginning, the first twenty years are the worst . . .

It is inevitable that comparisons will be made, if not by the parents, then by unenlightened teachers and perhaps by the children themselves. Unenlightened teachers can do a lot of harm, especially if you have twins and they are in the same class. You will probably have to go and see the teacher in the end and explain to her what she really ought to have discovered for herself (though admittedly, with forty in the class it must be difficult), that Peter and John are quite as intelligent as each other, just different, that's all.

Within the family there is always the play of one achievement against another. In families where the children are close together, the younger one will strive all the time to do what the older one does – and will often succeed. This can cause friction; or the older one expresses scorn at the younger one's effort: 'Pooh! That's not very good!' or 'Can't you do *that*? It's easy!' Boys have teased and girls have been 'catty' for a long time and it may be a few centuries yet before families achieve the kind of harmony that Chang Kung had in his. But if the older one makes hurtful remarks like the above, you can immediately deflate him by saying, 'Yes, but you did drawings like this when you were five. Don't you remember that terribly funny picture you drew of Daddy and everybody thought it was a cow?' – and laugh; better still if you have kept it and can bring it out to prove the point. There will be lots of merriment and everyone will be happy. Or you can jump in before derogatory remarks are even made: 'Oh, isn't that good! Aren't you clever? Look, isn't this pretty?'

– bringing the older one to admire. 'You used to make things like this when you were in Class I, didn't you? Now, what have *you* got to show me?'

Deep down, these frictions are caused by the desire (and need) of every child to feel significant and assured of his parents' love – especially his mother's – in the early years. We should do our best to bring out and encourage our children's gifts. Often they are quite different and there is no competition; and in music you can avoid this by having them each learn a different instrument. If you play an instrument too, this will lead, in time, to a family ensemble and can be great fun. Where their abilities converge it will be more difficult to find areas where each can shine in his or her own right; but at least we must try. Did we not say at the beginning that bringing up a family was the hardest, most demanding but also most rewarding job that anyone could undertake?

Difficult children

However hard we try, it is always possible to have a really difficult child in the family, one who causes us unending heartache and worry and drives us to our wits' end. One can see, as has already been said, that the propensities of character which can lead to delinquency are present in all children and they must be trained properly so that they learn to control the animal and develop the spiritual sides of their natures. Man has two natures and as long as we are on this plane we shall have a certain amount of tension between them. 'Abdu'l-Bahá says:

> In man there are two natures; his spiritual or higher nature and his material or lower nature. In one he approaches God, in the other he lives for the world alone. Signs of both these natures are to be found in men. In his material aspect he expresses untruth, cruelty and injustice; all these are the

outcome of his lower nature. The attributes of his Divine nature are shown forth in love, mercy, kindness, truth and justice, one and all being expressions of his higher nature. Every good habit, every noble quality belongs to man's spiritual nature, whereas all his imperfections and sinful actions are born of his material nature. If a man's Divine nature dominates his human nature, we have a saint.

Man has the power both to do good and to do evil; if his power for good predominates and his inclinations to do wrong are conquered, then man in truth may be called a saint.[24]

This volume is not intended to be a manual on child psychology, nor am I qualified to write with authority on this subject in any case. It is for the psychologists among us to study the Writings and enlarge in detail on their application in this field; but I believe that the Faith has the answer to every problem, including that of 'problem children'. In a Bahá'í world it is to be hoped that there will be no such problems – or at least not of the magnitude they are today; but parents cannot wait for the psychologists to write books. They want help *now*, and help there is in plenty, even on this subject. The answers are given by implication in everything we have discussed so far, but there are one or two passages dealing specifically with this matter which it might be helpful to include here. 'Abdu'l-Bahá says:

> The root cause of wrongdoing is ignorance, and we must therefore hold fast to the tools of perception and knowledge. Good character must be taught . . .[25]

The Master goes on to say what every social worker and child psychologist knows:

> It is extremely difficult to teach the individual and refine his character once puberty is passed. By then, as experience hath shown, even if every effort be exerted to modify some tendency of his, it all availeth nothing. He may, perhaps, improve

somewhat today; but let a few days pass and he forgetteth, and turneth backward to his habitual condition and accustomed ways. Therefore it is in early childhood that a firm foundation must be laid. While the branch is green and tender it can easily be made straight.[26]

The Guardian must have been asked frequently for advice on how to deal with difficult children. The following passages are replies sent to individual believers who requested such advice:

With regard to the statement attributed to 'Abdu'l-Bahá and which you have quoted in your letter regarding a 'problem child'; these statements of the Master, however true in their substance, should never be given a literal interpretation. 'Abdu'l-Bahá could have never meant that a child should be left to himself, entirely free. In fact Bahá'í education, just like any other system of education is based on the assumption that there are certain natural deficiencies in every child, no matter how gifted, which his educators, whether his parents, schoolmasters, or his spiritual guides and preceptors should endeavour to remedy. Discipline of some sort, whether physical, moral or intellectual, is indeed indispensable, and no training can be said to be complete and fruitful if it disregards this element. The child when born is far from being perfect. It is not only helpless, but actually is imperfect, and even is naturally inclined towards evil. He should be trained, his natural inclinations harmonized, adjusted and controlled, and if necessary suppressed or regulated, so as to ensure his healthy physical and moral development. Bahá'í parents cannot simply adopt an attitude of non-resistance towards their children, particularly those who are unruly and violent by nature. It is not even sufficient that they should pray on their behalf. Rather they should endeavour to inculcate, gently and patiently, into their youthful minds such principles of moral conduct and initiate them into the principles and teachings of the Cause with such tactful and loving care as would enable them to become 'true sons of God' and develop into loyal and intelligent citizens of His Kingdom. This is the high purpose which Bahá'u'lláh Himself has clearly defined as the chief goal of every education.[27]

He is sorry to hear your little boy is not developing satisfactorily; very few children are really bad. They do, however, sometimes have complicated personalities and need very wise handling to enable them to grow into normal, moral, happy adults. If you feel convinced your son will really benefit from going to Father Flanagan's school you could send him there. But in general we should certainly always avoid sending Bahá'í children to orthodox religious schools, especially Catholic, as the children receive the imprint of religious beliefs we as believers know are out-dated and no longer for this age. He will especially pray for the solution of this problem.[28]

Shoghi Effendi was deeply saddened to learn from your letter . . . of the rather serious situation which your daughter's conduct and her general attitude towards the Cause have created . . .

Although he highly deplores this fact, and is fully aware of the bad repercussions which it may have on the Cause, yet he feels that nothing short of your motherly care and love and of the counsels which you and the friends can give her, can effectively remedy this situation. Above all, you should be patient, and confident that your efforts to that end are being sustained and guided through the confirmations of Bahá'u'lláh. He is surely hearing your prayers, and will no doubt accept them, and thus hasten the gradual and complete materialization of your hopes and expectations for your daughter and for the Cause.

The Guardian would advise you, therefore, not to take any drastic action with regard to your daughter's attendance at the meetings . . . For in this way there is much greater chance to reform her character than through force or any other drastic method. Love and kindness have far greater influence than punishment upon the improvement of human character.

The Guardian, therefore, trusts that by this means you will succeed in gradually introducing a fundamental change in your daughter's life, and also in making of her a better and truer believer. He is fervently praying on her behalf that she may fully attain this station.[29]

The following beautiful prayer of 'Abdu'l-Bahá must have been written in response to an appeal on the part of the parents of just such a child:

> O Peerless Lord! Be Thou a shelter for this poor child and a kind and forgiving Master unto this erring and unhappy soul. O Lord! Though we are but worthless plants, yet we belong to Thy garden of roses. Though saplings without leaves and blossoms, yet we are a part of Thine orchard. Nurture this plant then through the outpourings of the clouds of Thy tender mercy and quicken and refresh this sapling through the reviving breath of Thy spiritual springtime. Suffer him to become heedful, discerning and noble and grant that he may attain eternal life and abide in Thy Kingdom for evermore.[30]

Consultation

The Guardian says, 'Consultation, frank and unfettered, is the bedrock of this order',[31] and this applies to the home just as much as to local spiritual assemblies. 'Abdu'l-Bahá tells us to

> Settle all things, both great and small, by consultation. Without prior consultation, take no important step in your own personal affairs. Concern yourselves with one another. Help along one another's projects and plans.[32]

Consultation on all that our children *can* be consulted about should start as soon as they are old enough to be consulted; but there are obviously areas where parents must have ultimate control, just as God, through His Manifestation, has ultimate control over us in certain matters. He says 'Be!' and it is, 'Thou shalt' and we do it. He does not consult us on matters where He knows better than we do what is good for us. So, for instance, you do not consult a child of three as to whether or not he should cross a busy main road by himself; but you might consult him about the advisability of putting his Paddington Bear to bed with his boots on.

Consultation does not imply that the parents should shirk their responsibilities and use it as a convenient method of hiding behind their children when they themselves are unwilling – or even perhaps afraid – to assert their authority or make up their own minds. One of the basic requirements of consultation is that one should know which spiritual principles are involved in the subject under discussion. We as parents have to teach these principles to our children; they cannot be expected to know them without being taught. Unless we do this, the likelihood is that they will be guided either by personal interest or by popular opinion. Sometimes the spiritual principles may be unpalatable or at least difficult to see the reason for; sometimes we ourselves may feel this too. Indeed, I would go so far as to suggest that what we find difficult to explain to others (and I don't just mean because we aren't eloquent), deep down in our heart of hearts we have not fully accepted ourselves. Children present us with all sorts of opportunities of coming to grips with such areas of uncertainty. When this happens, we should get the books out and study, and pray for illumination and strength. 'Abdu'l-Bahá says:

> Man must consult on all matters, whether major or minor, so that he may become cognizant of what is good.[33]

He goes on to explain the value of consultation:

> Consultation giveth him insight into things and enableth him to delve into questions which are unknown.[34]

If we balance this against His statement about meditation: that 'Through it affairs of which man knew nothing are unfolded before his eyes',[35] we have very good advice! So many young people – and grown-ups for that matter – speak first and think afterwards. Young people, who are usually in a hurry, find it very hard not to do this. 'Abdu'l-Bahá tells us:

> The light of truth shineth from the faces of those who engage in consultation. Such consultation causeth the living waters to flow in the meadows of man's reality, the rays of ancient glory to shine upon him, and the tree of his being to be adorned with wondrous fruit. The members who are consulting, however, should behave in the utmost love, harmony and sincerity towards each other.[36]

Consultation is a mature skill and one which even local spiritual assemblies don't always manage very well. It has to be learned the hard way; but it can begin in the home, where all members of the family have their rights. Indeed, the home is probably the most difficult of all areas in which this skill should be practised. The self-willed have to learn to submit to authority and majority wishes, the timid to overcome their desire to be told what to do all the time. Also, sheer politeness and good manners usually prevent us from expressing ourselves too rudely to other people, but in the home familiarity breeds contempt. To be able to control one's temper and put a zip fastener on one's mouth in the rough and tumble of home life is to have achieved something praiseworthy indeed! The following passage from Bahá'u'lláh is, I think, particularly apt in the home situation:

> It is Our wish and desire that every one of you may become a source of all goodness unto men, and an example of uprightness to mankind. Beware lest ye prefer yourselves above your neighbours. Fix your gaze upon Him Who is the Temple of God amongst men. He, in truth, hath offered up His life as a ransom for the redemption of the world. He, verily, is the All-

Bountiful, the Gracious, the Most High. If any differences arise amongst you, behold Me standing before your face, and overlook the faults of one another for My name's sake and as a token of your love for My manifest and resplendent Cause. We love to see you at all times consorting in amity and concord within the paradise of My good-pleasure, and to inhale from your acts the fragrance of friendliness and unity, of loving-kindness and fellowship. Thus counselleth you the All-Knowing, the Faithful. We shall always be with you; if We inhale the perfume of your fellowship, Our heart will assuredly rejoice, for naught else can satisfy Us. To this beareth witness every man of true understanding.[37]

Law and order

As we have said, the family is the basic unit of society. We should aim to make it happy and to make our children happy. This doesn't mean spoiling them – making them happy by giving in to them for the sake of peace and quiet. I personally don't believe a child *is* happy in this kind of situation. A child needs love, yes, but he also needs security, and this implies a framework of order and discipline so that he knows where he stands. One of the most important things we have to realise and pass on to our children is that although love and unity are divine qualities, they do not just happen by themselves because we are Bahá'ís. They have to be worked at. The Faith is not a wishy-washy, pie-in-the-sky affair. We are not a lot of invertebrates flopping about all over the place – and the Faith is not invertebrate either. We belong to the highest class of vertebrates: we have a backbone to keep us upright; and any religion worthy of the name must also have a backbone to keep its followers upright. Uprightness is a quality to be desired in man, both physically and spiritually. No country would last long without a firm structure of law and order. What makes us think that the

Kingdom of God, which *will* one day be a reality on earth as it is in heaven, can manage without one? It too must have law and order for its proper functioning. From the repressive, divine-right-of-fathers attitude of the nineteenth century the pendulum has swung to the opposite extreme of permissiveness. Neither is right and both lead to unhappiness and strife. Bahá'u'lláh says:

> They whom God hath endued with insight will readily recognize that the precepts laid down by God constitute the highest means for the maintenance of order in the world and the security of its peoples. He that turneth away from them, is accounted among the abject and foolish. We, verily, have commanded you to refuse the dictates of your evil passions and corrupt desires, and not to transgress the bounds which the Pen of the Most High hath fixed, for these are the breath of life unto all created things.[38]

We have to come to a realisation that the laws which Bahá'u'lláh has given to us, whether personal or social in nature, are what we need for our spiritual and social development. We may not always like them or understand the reason for them; we may find it hard to obey them. Our doctor's medicine is not always pleasant to take, but it does make us better. Submission to the Will of the Divine Physician also brings its rewards. Bahá'u'lláh says:

> O ye peoples of the world! Know assuredly that My commandments are the lamps of My loving providence among My servants, and the keys of My mercy for My creatures. Thus hath it been sent down from the heaven of the Will of your Lord, the Lord of Revelation. Were any man to taste the sweetness of the words which the lips of the All-Merciful have willed to utter, he would, though the treasures of the earth be in his possession, renounce them one and all, that he might vindicate the truth of even one of His commandments, shining above the day spring of His bountiful care and loving-kindness.
> Say: From My laws the sweet smelling savour of My garment

can be smelled, and by their aid the standards of victory will be planted upon the highest peaks. The Tongue of My power hath, from the heaven of My omnipotent glory, addressed to My creation these words: 'Observe My commandments, for the love of My beauty.' Happy is the lover that hath inhaled the divine fragrance of his Best-Beloved from these words, laden with the perfume of a grace which no tongue can describe. By My life! He who hath drunk the choice wine of fairness from the hands of My bountiful favour, will circle around My commandments that shine above the Day Spring of My creation.

Think not that We have revealed unto you a mere code of laws. Nay, rather, We have unsealed the choice Wine with the fingers of might and power. To this beareth witness that which the Pen of Revelation hath revealed. Meditate upon this, O men of insight! . . .[39]

After such an exalted explanation of their spiritual significance we can hardly be in any doubt that they are very far from being a 'mere code of laws'! They are not just whims and fancies of Bahá'u'lláh. He did not, as it were, simply go into His study, sit down at His desk, pick up His pen, scratch His head and say, 'Now I will reveal laws for the world.' They are part of Revelation and as such, come from God. If we will obey these laws, we shall often find out *why* we should obey them. As Christ said, 'If any man will do his will, he shall know of the doctrine, whether it be of God, or whether I speak of myself.'[40]

We must help our children to react as Bahá'ís and we can only do this if we react as Bahá'ís ourselves first. That is, when confronted with any decision of morals or ethics, however small it may be, to know immediately which teaching or principle of Bahá'u'lláh underlies the situation and have the courage to act on it. 'Practice makes perfect,' they say, and if we go on doing this long enough, a time will come when there is no decision to be made, because there just isn't any alternative to the right one. As Saint

Augustine put it, 'Love (God) and do what you like.'[41] If we love God we shall like what He likes and act accordingly. This thought is expressed by Bahá'u'lláh in more than one prayer:

By Thy glory! I wish only what Thou wishest, and cherish what Thou cherishest.[42]

By Thy Most Great Name, O Thou Lord of all nations! I have desired only what Thou didst desire, and love only what Thou dost love.[43]

All this needs to be taught with wisdom. Our children need to know how to strike the balance between enjoying the benefits of this world – which Bahá'u'lláh says are not forbidden to us as Bahá'ís[44] – and the standards of the Faith. One might usefully discuss with them, for instance, how one obeys an absolute prohibition with moderation, or at what point moderation becomes compromise. The Bahá'í Faith is not an ascetic religion, nor are we expected to become hermits. In a world where people immediately react to, say, the fact that one doesn't drink alcohol, with the assumption that one thereby thinks one is better than they are, great wisdom is required in how to handle such a situation when one is faced with it. It also takes time to find out for oneself that God 'will aid every one that aideth Him',[45] when one refuses to compromise one's principles for the sake of being popular, even in such mundane things as this. In time one comes to *know* this, but to begin with it takes courage not to shrink from speaking out.

Maturity at fifteen

The coming of age of the human race means the coming of age first of the individuals who comprise it. Maturity does not come all at once in every direction, and perhaps it is fitting that the kind of maturity which we seek to bring about in the world before all else – spiritual maturity – is the kind which Bahá'u'lláh says comes at the age of fifteen. Therefore we can assure our young adolescents that, at fifteen, they are perfectly capable of making a significant contribution towards the spiritualisation of the human race. They do not have to wait until they are mature in other ways. The Guardian wrote as long ago as 1935:

> The problem with which you are faced is one which concerns and seriously puzzles many of our present-day youth. How to attain spirituality is, indeed, a question to which every young man and woman must sooner or later try to find a satisfactory answer. It is precisely because no such satisfactory answer has been given or found, that modern youth finds itself bewildered, and is being consequently carried away by the materialistic forces that are so powerfully undermining the foundation of man's moral and spiritual life.
> Indeed, the chief reason for the evils now rampant in society is the lack of spirituality. The materialistic civilization of our age has so much absorbed the energy and interest of mankind that people in general do no longer feel the necessity of raising themselves above the forces and conditions of their daily material existence. There is not sufficient demand for things that we should call spiritual to differentiate them from the needs and requirements of our physical existence.
> The universal crisis affecting mankind is, therefore, essentially spiritual in its causes. The spirit of the age, taken on the whole, is irreligious. Man's outlook on life is too crude and materialistic to enable him to elevate himself into the higher realms of the spirit.
> It is this condition, so sadly morbid, into which society has fallen, that religion seeks to improve and transform. For the core of religious faith is that mystic feeling which unites man with God. This state of spiritual communion can be brought about and maintained by means of meditation and prayer. And this is the reason why Bahá'u'lláh has so much stressed the importance of worship. It is not sufficient for a believer merely

to accept and observe the teachings. He should, in addition, cultivate the sense of spirituality which he can acquire chiefly by means of prayer. The Bahá'í Faith, like all other Divine Religions, is thus fundamentally mystic in character. Its chief goal is the development of the individual and society, through the acquisition of spiritual virtues and powers. It is the soul of man which has first to be fed. And this spiritual nourishment prayer can best provide. Laws and institutions, as viewed by Bahá'u'lláh, can become really effective only when our inner spiritual life has been perfected and transformed. Otherwise religion will degenerate into a mere organization, and become a dead thing.

The believers, particularly the young ones, should, therefore, fully realize the necessity of praying. For prayer is absolutely indispensable to their inner spiritual development, and this, as already stated, is the very foundation and purpose of the religion of God.[46]

Other kinds of maturity may take longer to achieve, but spiritual maturity is within our grasp at what we may think is a surprisingly tender age. Could it, I wonder, be connected with the idea that unless we become as little children, we shall not enter the Kingdom of Heaven?

Children seem to remain unsophisticated – some would say innocent – for shorter and shorter lengths of time as the generations pass. If maturity is to come at fifteen in the future, this is in some senses inevitable; but I think that it should be our aim to teach them in such a way that they will retain a delight in simple things, and that quality of childlikeness which Christ said was essential for entry into the Kingdom of Heaven.[47] He did not mean child*ish*ness, which is not a pleasant quality in an adult or even in a youngster of fifteen. The word 'childlike' has a positive ring about it, and surely includes things like wonder, trust, love and an acceptance of what comes.

Maturity also implies, I think, the acceptance and

appreciation of differences. 'Abdu'l-Bahá teaches us that differences do exist, whatever some political and educational theory may imagine to the contrary:

> It is evident that although education improves the morals of mankind, confers the advantages of civilization and elevates man from lowest degrees to the station of sublimity, there is nevertheless a difference in the intrinsic or natal capacity of individuals. Ten children of the same age, with equal station of birth, taught in the same school, partaking of the same food, in all respects subject to the same environment, their interests equal and in common, will evidence separate and distinct degrees of capability and advancement; some exceedingly intelligent and progressive, some of mediocre ability, others limited and incapable. One may become a learned professor while another under the same course of education proves dull and stupid. From all standpoints the opportunities have been equal but the results and outcomes vary from the highest to lowest degree of advancement. It is evident therefore that mankind differs in natal capacity and intrinsic intellectual endowment. Nevertheless, although capacities are not the same, every member of the human race is capable of education.[48]

As Bahá'ís we are in a good position to be able to lead the way in appreciating the true worth of every individual. Because we are called by God and not by man, we are constantly being presented with apparently unmixable mixtures and made to get on with it: different races, different age groups, different social backgrounds, different languages and different experiences, having to function harmoniously together in the same community and on the same local spiritual assembly. We need to help our children on the one hand to admire, respect and look up to those more gifted than themselves, and on the other to appreciate the talents – which may not be immediately apparent – of those who may not be gifted in the way the world sees and rewards things. We need to teach them to encourage, not condemn; to understand, not despise; that man is a 'mine rich in gems of inestimable value'.[49] Sometimes open-cast mining is not enough. One has to dig deeply in order to find the gems.

The one-Bahá'í-parent family

I would like to offer a word of encouragement to those Bahá'ís who do not have the support of their husband or wife. Some non-Bahá'í spouses are sympathetic and are quite happy for their Bahá'í partner to attend meetings and bring up the children in the Faith. The guiding principle here is discretion: knowing what it is vital that you should do and which meetings you should attend, and where you should consider your partner's needs as more important. In their letter of 17 April 1981 the Universal House of Justice says, 'If the believer is the only one of his family who has embraced the Faith, it is his duty to endeavour to lead as many other family members as possible to the light of divine guidance.' To describe it as a 'duty' is to emphasise its importance; to require the believer to 'lead' is to give guidance as to how this duty is to be performed. Coercion is not to be indulged in. As regards the observance of one's Bahá'í obligations, due consultation will usually remove any little difficulties that may arise. The Guardian advised as follows:

> The question of the training and education of children in case one of the parents is a non-Bahá'í is one which solely concerns the parents themselves, who should decide about it the way they find best and most conducive to the maintenance of the unity of their family, and to the future welfare of their children. Once the child comes of age, however, he should be given full freedom to choose his religion, irrespective of the wishes and desires of his parents.[50]

I am much more concerned with those friends whose

husbands or wives – though more often the former, I think – make it difficult for them to fulfil their obligations, one of which is to bring up their children in the Faith. In extreme cases, where promises are exacted, you will have to respect your husband's wishes and not talk of the Faith to your children. One lady I know had this situation for nineteen years until her husband died. Both children, through their own investigation, subsequently became Bahá'ís; but their mother, who is a very lovely person and a devoted Bahá'í, must have prayed and shed many tears in private. She was later rewarded by seeing her son and daughter active in the Faith – a living example of Bahá'u'lláh's words:

Say: Await ye till God will have changed His favour unto you. Nothing whatsoever escapeth Him. He knoweth the secrets both of the heavens and of the earth. His knowledge embraceth all things . . . He, verily, shall increase the reward of them that endure with patience.[51]

Most Bahá'ís do not have to put up with a situation as bad as this; but even so, it sometimes takes a great deal of courage, determination and loving perseverance to remain steadfast in the face of opposition or lack of understanding, of indifference or even ridicule. The temptation to give up trying under such circumstances must be strong, but if you have faith in the sustaining power of God and cling tenaciously to the cord of His mercy; and if you gently but firmly explain that the Faith means everything to you and there are some things you absolutely must do and some meetings you just do have to go to, your partner will probably surprise you by accepting the situation with a better grace than you thought possible – and respecting you more into the bargain; and if your partner wants the children to go to church as well as to Bahá'í meetings, there is no reason why they should not do so as far as the Bahá'ís are concerned.

It would be impossible to suggest ways of handling this situation, as it affects the upbringing of the children, which would be applicable in every case. The father's beliefs (or lack of them), his prejudices, his attitudes to life in general and family life in particular, his attitude to women (which will affect his relationship with his wife), his habits and his temperament will vary from father to father. What has been said so far is general in nature because of this; to be of any help further, it would be necessary to know the particular circumstances of the mother's situation, and this is clearly impossible. The things that all mothers can do in common (and fathers too, if the situation is reversed) are to accept the will of God, believing that there is a reason for what is happening and that 'nothing save that which will profit them can befall My loved ones',[52] to pray, to have unwavering faith and to be patient and wait. The power of all these things together is far greater than any of us realises. 'Abdu'l-Bahá, in response to a question put to Him in America in 1912 by a little Jewish girl whose problems were threatening to overwhelm her, said,

> To pray is to trust in God and to be submissive in all things to Him. Be submissive, then things will change for you. Put your family in God's hands. Love God's will. Strong ships are not conquered by the sea; they ride the waves! Now be a strong ship, not a battered one.[53]

There can be no more encouraging advice than this.

It is interesting to note what 'Abdu'l-Bahá says about the family where only one parent is a Bahá'í:

> Consider that if the mother is a believer, the children will become believers too, even if the father denieth the Faith; while, if the mother is not a believer, the children are deprived of faith,

even if the father be a believer convinced and firm. Such is the usual outcome, except in rare cases.[54]

At the time the Master said this, male domination in the home, even in the West, was much more widespread than it is today, and if the father did not want his children to be brought up as Bahá'ís, there was not much the mother could do about it except pray. Of course, it is not *always* true that where the mother is a Bahá'í the children will become Bahá'ís. There are so many imponderables in this matter that it would be quite impossible to say why this happens in some families and not in others. Perhaps fathers can take comfort from the fact that the Master says 'is' and not 'will always be' – and see this statement as a challenge. They may like to consider the possibility of taking up the challenge and prove that He did not mean His statement to apply for ever. Perhaps it requires that fathers develop more of the qualities usually attributed to women – gentleness, patience, long-suffering, loving-kindness, spirituality – and assume the mother's rôle of supervising the children's morning and evening reading and prayers, teaching by example the Divine Standard of behaviour, as did the beloved Master Himself.

Happiness

But when all is said and done, the thing we surely most want our children to feel about their religion is happiness. If they (and we) are happy in it they will be more likely to accept its restraints with radiant acquiescence. When I was young, my mother used several little books of nightly readings and prayers at my bedtime and several of the quotations contained in them sank in and became part of my thinking. One such saying I remember, though I cannot tell you now who said it; it has remained with me, I think, because it rings true: 'If your morals make you dreary, depend upon it they are wrong.'

Let us teach our children to praise and thank God for His bounty. In the same way that the Bahá'í prayers begin and end in God, so should our every day begin and end in God, especially in praise and gratitude. Blessings pour down on the soul that is grateful – and that includes gratitude for the things we don't like as well as those we do.

Bahá'u'lláh loved flowers and nice things. His granddaughter gives us an insight into what He felt:

> He was always punctual, and loved daintiness and order.
>
> He was very particular and refined in his personal arrangements, and liked to see everybody well groomed, and as neatly dressed as possible. Above all things, cleanliness was desirable to Him.
>
> 'Why not put on your prettiest frocks?' He would say to us.[55]

The way we dress, especially for Feasts and Holy Days, the way we keep our homes, cultivate our gardens and so on, has its effect on the children, because deep down these things proclaim to them what we feel about our religion. In His Tablet on purity 'Abdu'l-Bahá tells us that although cleanliness is only a physical thing, it has a great effect on spirituality.[56] Beauty can be thought of as a kind of visual cleanliness. There is no virtue in continuing to be a rough diamond once you know how to become polished. Attractive physical surroundings do help towards a spiritual atmosphere: why else should the Guardian have made the Holy Places in Israel so beautiful? Once more we are back to how much it means to us.

Let us teach our children to be happy with simple things and not demand too much in life; to take a delight in finding the first snowdrop, or hearing the song of a blackbird on a spring evening; to appreciate the little kindnesses that friends and neighbours do for them – and to go out of their way in their turn to do small kindnesses for other people; to be helpful about the house and to undertake their appointed tasks with a good grace. In other words, to be content. Indeed, this may be the most blessed gift we can give them today, when so many people belong to 'the gimme and grabbit brigade', as I once heard it described; to be able to do things for the love of doing them – which is another way of saying for the love of God – without expecting financial or confectionary reward all the time. Bahá'u'lláh sums up this attitude of wonder and contentment when He says:

. . . whatever is in the heavens and whatever is on the earth is a direct evidence of the revelation within it of the attributes and names of God, inasmuch as within every atom are enshrined the signs that bear eloquent testimony to the revelation of that most great Light. Methinks, but for the potency of that revelation, no being could ever exist. How resplendent the luminaries of knowledge that shine in an atom, and how vast the oceans of wisdom that surge within a drop![57]

A positive attitude to life

Let us give our children a positive attitude to life – a vision that will never leave them; a vision of a future world commonwealth towards which we are all working; a vision of service to humanity that will enable them to see beyond personal problems in whatever vicissitudes may fall to their lot in life.

Above all, let us try to give our children the only thing that will make their lives meaningful, bring everlasting joy to them and sustain them in time of trouble – love for God, for Bahá'u'lláh and the Master; so well expressed in the words of what used to be my favourite hymn before I became a Bahá'í:

Fill thou my life, O Lord my God,
In every part with praise,
That my whole being may proclaim
Thy being and thy ways.

Not for the lip of praise alone,
Nor e'en the praising heart,
I ask, but for a life made up
Of praise in every part:

Praise in the common words I speak,
Life's common looks and tones,
In intercourse at hearth or board
With my belovèd ones.

Fill every part of me with praise:
Let all my being speak
Of thee and of thy love, O Lord,
Poor though I be and weak.

So shall no part of day or night
From sacredness be free;
But all my life, in every step,
Be fellowship with thee.[58]

5

First Teach Your Own Self

Set the example

It goes without saying that if we want our children to become good Bahá'ís we have to set the example. Bahá'u'lláh says:

God hath prescribed unto every one the duty of teaching His Cause. Whoever ariseth to discharge this duty, must needs, ere he proclaimeth His Message, adorn himself with the ornament of an upright and praiseworthy character, so that his words may attract the hearts of such as are receptive to his call. Without it, he can never hope to influence his hearers.[1]

Well, we know this, but we probably tend to think of it more in connection with teaching our friends than with teaching our own children. But they are our severest critics. They are clear-sighted and devastatingly logical in their thinking and we do not deceive *them*! Our behaviour is their book and they do not need a magnifying glass to read it. They know very clearly what we should be like:

Whoso ariseth among you to teach the Cause of his Lord, let him, before all else, teach his own self, that his speech may attract the hearts of them that hear him. Unless he teacheth his own self, the words of his mouth will not influence the heart of the seeker.[2]

Then there is that humorous dig at human weakness:

> Take heed, O people, lest ye be of them that give good counsel to others but forget to follow it themselves.[3]

For if we don't practise what we preach, our offspring, as well as quite an array of heavenly realities, will bring against us the accusation of falsehood.

We have seen that, as 'Abdu'l-Bahá tells us, 'Truthfulness is the foundation of all human virtues.'[4] Integrity could be seen as the expression of this virtue in our daily relationships with others. Those closest to us know beyond any shadow of doubt how well our example measures up to our precept.

Love humanity

> If thou wishest to guide the souls, it is incumbent on thee to be firm, to be good, and to be imbued with praiseworthy attributes and divine qualities under all circumstances. Be a sign of love, a manifestation of mercy, a fountain of tenderness, kind-hearted, good to all, and gentle to the servants of God, and especially to those who bear relation to thee, both men and women. Bear every ordeal that befalleth thee from the people, and confront them not save with kindness, with great love and good wishes.[5]

The oneness of mankind is the pivotal principle of the Faith. The distinctive character of Bahá'í life revolves around it. Our attitude to the people we meet, especially those from overseas, our hospitality, the pleasure of our partaking in what it is to be hoped is a happy and busy community life, all reflect our attitude. Again, 'Abdu'l-Bahá says:

> Be thou loving to every afflicted one, a dispeller of sorrows to every grieved one, a refuge to every fearful one, a heavenly food to every destitute one, a balm to every wounded one, a consolation to dejected hearts, a blessing to unfortunate souls, a treasure to every begging one, and a succor to every lamenting one – so that thou mayest be a banner of guidance and the

essence of piety among the maid-servants of Thy Supreme Lord. Verily, thy Lord is the Beneficent, the Gracious, the Bestower!⁶

It may be harder for older people coming into the Faith to rid themselves of prejudices inculcated in them in childhood, but all must try. Freedom from prejudice must be deliberately cultivated. The Guardian says:

> It should be deliberately cultivated through the various and every-day opportunities, no matter how insignificant, that present themselves, whether in their homes, their business offices, their schools and colleges, their social parties and recreation grounds, their Bahá'í meetings, conferences, conventions, summer schools and Assemblies.⁷

It is in our unguarded moments, or when we think the children aren't listening, that we reveal the true nature of our attitudes. Let us strive that they may become such that we would *not* be ashamed to be caught voicing them in such unguarded moments.

Implications

We read Bahá'u'lláh's famous passage beginning 'Be generous in prosperity and thankful in adversity . . .'⁸ and we think how marvellous it is. I suspect that we do not fully appreciate its implications. Our *aim* is the spiritualisation of the whole world but each one of us can really only operate in a very small sphere – our own immediate surroundings. This means the family, the neighbours and the people we work with. We have enough on our plates if we manage successfully to obey 'Abdu'l-Bahá's instructions, given in His Will and Testament. These have already been quoted but it will do no harm to quote them again:

> Should other peoples and nations be unfaithful to you show

your fidelity unto them, should they be unjust toward you show justice towards them, should they keep aloof from you attract them to yourself, should they show their enmity be friendly towards them, should they poison your lives sweeten their souls, should they inflict a wound upon you be a salve to their sores. Such are the attributes of the sincere! Such are the attributes of the truthful.[9]

It is no use talking in grand terms about uniting mankind and not being able to live in unity and peace with those around us. There is a well-known saying, 'Charity begins at home.' For us Bahá'ís, perhaps it could be altered slightly: 'Unity begins at home.'

'It matters' and 'I care'

In the end I think it boils down to two simple ideas which we need to get across to our children, very much by example as well as precept: 'It matters' and 'I care'. How often does one hear people say, when something they haven't done very well is pointed out to them, 'Oh well, it doesn't matter', or 'Who cares?' We have to teach our children that it *does* matter – down to the last detail – and that nothing but the best they can offer is good enough for the Faith; that if they take a job on, they should see it through to the end (including the tidying up) and not give up half-way through when it becomes tedious. Excellence in *all* things. They need to develop the quality of stickability. In this way they can change 'tedium' into 'Te Deum'.* If they can see things like this, then doing their homework or practising or their jobs about the house becomes praise to God; and with the beloved Master holding their hands and laughingly encouraging them to

---

* *Te Deum laudamus* – 'We praise Thee, O God'. This hymn, in the Book of Common Prayer of the Church of England, is usually referred to as 'The Te Deum'.

try harder, how can they fail? For this is a day of VERY GREAT THINGS![10]

Training is necessary to excel in anything. I have always thought that the parable of the talents[11] is most applicable in this context, because the English word has two meanings. Christ approved of the servants who put their talents to good use and developed them, not the one whose attitude was 'I haven't got very much, so I won't bother; it doesn't matter'. It *always* matters. One can *always* improve. We should encourage our children to *want* to improve, whether it is, say, in lettering and layout, so that they can produce better posters advertising Bahá'í meetings, or in the mastering of a fault in their characters.

Where character is concerned, let us teach our children to become responsible for their own and want to improve them. All of us, as we have already said, are engaged in this struggle and there is never an end to it. So much modern thinking seems to veer away from accepting responsibility for one's actions and towards the 'I'm made like this so you can take it or leave it' attitude, or tracing one's faults back to something that happened to one in early childhood, as if that were all that needed to be said on the matter. As Bahá'ís, we cannot make such excuses, because we have the Divine Standard constantly before us, to which we must try to conform ourselves, and we have the Perfect Exemplar to look up to, Who is bidding us all the time to 'come up higher'.[12] In this connection, I have always found it helpful, not just to ask myself 'What would 'Abdu'l-Bahá do?', but 'What would 'Abdu'l-Bahá do if He were I?' We simply cannot take the line that somebody else can be blamed for the things we do.

How much does it mean to us?

We should try to do things together as far as possible. If

we are in a community, Holy Days and Feasts should be happy community occasions; if we are isolated, we should still celebrate them and do something special on those days; so that in both cases the children come to associate them with happiness. We shall have more to say on this subject in the next chapter. In the matter of attending meetings, however, there are two pitfalls into which we may stumble if we aren't careful: one is under-doing it and the other is over-doing it. Both are dangerous and should be avoided.

As for under-doing it: do we always put the Faith first? If we truly love God, it will be natural for us to put attendance at a Nineteen Day Feast or Holy Day before anything else that may crop up on that date. When asked if we would like to go round to the neighbours, go to the cinema, a dance, or whatever it is, it becomes second nature to say, 'Sorry, I can't. I've got a Bahá'í meeting tonight.' Children are quick to pick up atmosphere and if going to the Feast is a bore to us they will find it a bore also. If we take the line, when called upon to make a decision of priorities, 'Oh bother, I can't go – there's an L.S.A. tonight', our children are likely to sulk at being 'dragged away from their play' to attend a children's class. If friends suddenly arrive on the doorstep when we are just about to set out, and instead of saying, 'I'm terribly sorry, I can't ask you in: we're just going to a meeting', we act on the impulse that it would be so *rude* to turn them away (though it might be a different story if it were the price of two theatre tickets which had to be sacrificed by staying at home!), our children will get the idea that the Faith can be put aside quite easily whenever it is inconvenient. Our actions shout much louder than words: if, instead of having the room ready and quiet in anticipation of the friends' arrival for the Feast, we don't turn the television off until the last moment (or even beyond!) because we don't want to miss an episode of our favourite serial, the children will soon decide which god we really worship and they will learn to worship it too; and if we are found choosing the readings for the Feast while the friends are arriving, which means we have not considered it sufficiently important to give it the concentration it requires beforehand, then they will also come to think that the Faith is not important.

Becoming familiar with the pattern of Bahá'í life takes time. The calendar has to be re-learnt. Mistakes are sometimes made because this pattern and calendar have not yet become deeply implanted in our consciousness. One way we can help ourselves to establish this consciousness is to buy a diary as soon as they appear in the shops each year and fill in all the Bahá'í dates for the following year, including any national events like Convention and Teaching Conference, World Religion Day and our Area Convention, whose dates we have been given or which we know always happen at certain weekends. If we do this we are less likely to make a date nearer the time and then find it conflicts with a Bahá'í religious obligation. Bahá'í diaries are better still, of course, but they are not always available, unfortunately, and even when they are, they are not in sufficient numbers. They often appear too late to be helpful, at least in the early part of the Christian year – for most Westerners still tend to think in terms of January 1st rather than Naw-Rúz. To have Bahá'í diaries available at a reasonable cost and in sufficient numbers for all Bahá'ís to have one would certainly help to solve this problem.

As for over-doing it: we can just as easily make mistakes in this direction and try to rationalise. We need to be honest with ourselves and examine our motives in taking small children to meetings which aren't really suitable for them and where they will disturb other people. Perhaps we are sometimes guilty of sacrificing our children on the altar of our own spiritual self-indulgence: expecting them to sit quietly through grown-up meetings when they ought to be in bed, telling ourselves that we want them 'to absorb the atmosphere', when what is really happening is that we ourselves don't want to miss anything. Even with the Feast, we should think very carefully about whether or not to bring them. We may wish to obey the Master's instruction to bring children to the Feast, even if they don't understand what is going on; but if we know that our toddlers are more likely to disturb the atmosphere and thus spoil it, not only for us parents – who won't be able to concentrate – but also for everyone else, we may feel the time has come for one of us to stay at home with them. We want our children to associate the Feast with happiness, not with a boring meeting at which they understand nothing and are thoroughly miserable. We all know our own children and every couple has to make their own decision in this matter; but the one thing we want to avoid at all costs is doing something which may produce an adverse reaction to the Faith later. It is one thing to teach our children thoroughly, but it is quite another to subject them to unhappiness of this sort. We have to decide whether or not they will sometimes absorb a more spiritual atmosphere asleep in their beds than by being tired, bored and fractious in a meeting.

Standards of decency, dignity and reverence

Reverence is a beautiful quality, to be admired and sought after. If we have reverence we are more likely to have decency and dignity than if we have not; but in so far as babies, when they are born, are not aware of God and do not know what is considered decent or dignified, they have to be taught these things. Here again, the best teacher is example. So let us be sure that, as parents, we observe decency in our appearance and speech, dignity in our behaviour and reverence in our attitude to God and His Manifestation.

As has been said, we should teach our children to show kindness to animals and have what Albert Schweitzer calls 'reverence for life'.* It is interesting that kindness to animals is one of the long list of attributes which Bahá'u'lláh says are desirable in the seeker after truth;[13] but He also adds, significantly, 'how much more unto his fellow-man, to him who is endowed with the power of utterance'.[14]

Standards of decency, dignity and reverence are outlined for us by Shoghi Effendi in *The Advent of Divine Justice*, pages 18–34. They deal with rectitude of conduct, a chaste and holy life, and the racial issue. All are important, but as parents perhaps we should study particularly pages 24–8, which deal with the meaning and implications of a chaste and holy life. The passages I am concerned with here are as follows:

> A chaste and holy life must be made the controlling principle in the behavior and conduct of all Bahá'ís, both in their social relations with the members of their own community, and in their contact with the world at large. It must adorn and reinforce the ceaseless labors and meritorious exertions of those whose enviable position is to propagate the Message, and to administer the affairs, of the Faith of Bahá'u'lláh. It must be upheld, in all its integrity and implications, in every phase of the life of those who fill the ranks of that Faith, whether in their homes, their travels, their clubs, their societies, their entertainments, their schools, and their universities. It must be accorded special consideration in the conduct of the social activities of every Bahá'í summer school and any other occasions on which Bahá'í community life is organized and fostered. It must be closely and continually identified with the mission of the Bahá'í

---

* See footnote on p. 55.

Youth, both as an element in the life of the Bahá'í community, and as a factor in the future progress and orientation of the youth of their own country.

Such a chaste and holy life, with its implications of modesty, purity, temperance, decency, and clean-mindedness, involves no less than the exercise of moderation in all that pertains to dress, language, amusements, and all artistic and literary avocations. It demands daily vigilance in the control of one's carnal desires and corrupt inclinations. It calls for the abandonment of a frivolous conduct, with its excessive attachment to trivial and often misdirected pleasures. It requires total abstinence from all alcoholic drinks, from opium, and from similar habit-forming drugs. It condemns the prostitution of art and of literature, the practices of nudism and of companionate marriage, infidelity in marital relationships, and all manner of promiscuity, of easy familiarity, and of sexual vices. It can tolerate no compromise with the theories, the standards, the habits, and the excesses of a decadent age. Nay rather it seeks to demonstrate, through the dynamic force of its example, the pernicious character of such theories, the falsity of such standards, the hollowness of such claims, the perversity of such habits, and the sacrilegious character of such excesses.[15]

Shoghi Effendi states that this passage is addressed mainly, though not entirely, to the Youth. We should read it carefully with our adolescent children, think about it together and try to help them to apply it in their own circumstances. We all *think* we know what it means, but I have a feeling that sometimes we let these high-sounding phrases go right over our heads and we don't *really* relate them in any detail to our own everyday life. For instance, what *is* clean-mindedness? What *is* the prostitution of art and literature? Do they have any connection with the jokes we laugh at, the books we read, the magazines we look at, the films and plays we go and see, the music we listen to, or the programmes we watch on the all-pervasive television? Do we always know what our children are absorbing from this most subtle and insinuating of influences in modern life? Do we always know if it is suitable for them? – and if we find that they have seen something whose moral standards are not acceptable to us as Bahá'ís, do we attempt to put them right? So much that we know to be wrong is portrayed as normal today, and regrettably, a lot of it is so. For instance, some of the soap operas so popular with television viewers are quite unsuitable for children and I am frankly horrified to think what effect they must be having on their minds during their most impressionable years. The attitudes and behaviour which some of them portray – with considerable sophistication and glitter – are bound to have their effect when absorbed as normal diet week after week. Adults may be able to laugh and say, 'It's rubbish,' but young children have no yardstick yet to enable them to make such a judgment. A materialistic and amoral philosophy screams at them from almost everything they see and hear outside the home. Let us try to ensure that, within it, they see and hear only that which is pure and good.

6

Feasts and Holy Days

The centre of our worship

Educating our children in the Faith is not just a matter of giving them the Teachings; it is also a matter of practising the 'observances of Bahá'í life' and its 'religious obligations'.[1] Attendance at Nineteen Day Feasts and Holy Day celebrations is of supreme importance. It ensures that we obtain regularly that spiritual food which is as necessary for our souls' growth as material food is for our bodies or human education for our minds. One day, there will no doubt be a House of Worship in every village to help us in the development of our spiritual life but for the foreseeable future the Feasts and Holy Days will be the main source of our worship for most of us.

Just as the Communion Service is the centre of their worship to Christians, so the Nineteen Day Feast, though quite different in character, is the centre of their worship to Bahá'ís. Indeed, 'Abdu'l-Bahá says that if the Feast is arranged in the way it should be, 'that supper is the "Lord's supper", for the result is the same result and the effect is the same effect'.[2] Although it is not a law to attend Feasts, Shoghi Effendi says we should 'consider it a duty and a privilege to be present on such occasions'.[3] Quite apart from the spiritual benefit missed if we are not present, there are other aspects of it which should not be underestimated. One is keeping up with the news, both local and national – and sometimes international; the other is taking part in the consultation, our opportunity to make suggestions and to have a say in what goes on. Indeed, if we are not members of the assembly, or are Youth or children, the consultation at the Feast is our only opportunity to take part in the decision-making process. We cannot complain at decisions arrived at by the assembly, based on recommendations made at the Feast, if we do not exercise our right to express our views. This is one of the religious innovations of the Faith – the privilege and duty of every member of the community, of whatever age, to consult about its affairs at the grass-roots level and in a spiritual atmosphere. It is therefore a great gift that has been given to us and we should not deprive ourselves of it. Added to this, we also get to know the members of our community, which is essential if we are to exercise our right to vote in a responsible manner at the Riḍván election of our local spiritual assembly.

If we are in a community, the proper arrangement of the Feast devolves upon the assembly and it is its responsibility to see that the arrangement is 'meet and seemly';[4] but it will help the assembly in the prosecution of this duty if all members of the community have the right attitude towards the Feast. There is no need to enlarge on this here; the Master's Tablets, given in the compilation *Seeking the Light of the Kingdom*,* describe this quite clearly.

In a community where there are problems of attendance, be it with parents with small children or old people who cannot or do not want to go out at night, especially in the dark, the assembly should find ways of helping. One of the responsibilities of local spiritual assemblies, listed by the Guardian, is that

---

* This compilation by the Universal House of Justice is also published under the title *Bahá'í Meetings: The Nineteen Day Feast*.

They must endeavour to promote amity and concord amongst the Friends, efface every lingering trace of distrust, coolness, and estrangement from every heart, and secure in its stead an active and wholehearted co-operation for the service of the Cause.[5]

Being able to attend Feasts is a very important factor in maintaining this amity and concord. We parents may also have valuable suggestions to make as to how the assembly can meet the various needs of the community in this respect. We might suggest (if it isn't done already) that they rotate the Feast venue, so that it is not always the same people who can't come; perhaps they could organise a baby-sitting service, so that parents who normally take it in turns to attend, can occasionally come along together. We might also suggest that whoever is choosing the readings be asked to think well ahead and send the references to those who they know cannot attend on that particular night. In this way, everyone can be present in spirit, if not in person. Afterwards, it would be greatly appreciated if someone were to take the news to such people and maybe the flowers and some of the refreshments. If this be done, the absent friends keep in touch and maintain the regular habit of the Feast every nineteen days. There is no need simply to sit down under our difficulties and say, 'I can't come.' We can prove the old saying, 'Love will find out a way.'

If we have small children and have decided not to bring them, we might suggest to the assembly that, occasionally, when the Feast falls on a Saturday or Sunday before sunset, it could be held in the afternoon and be geared to the children: that is, the readings and prayers should be chosen with small children in mind and so kept very simple and short. When this is done, it is not only the children who benefit; adults, too, sometimes find a short thought easier to take in than a long one! Provided this is done only occasionally, it can be extremely helpful in the education of our children. If we have laid a foundation of quiet attention during their prayers at home, they will be more likely to sit quietly and attend for the brief period of time needed on an occasion such as this. They are thus being gently prepared for reverent and dignified behaviour when they are old enough to attend all the Feasts.

All that has been said so far applies equally well to Holy Days, though here the problem is not so acute. There is no lengthy period of consultation on matters which are above their heads, and the whole thing is quite different. Holy Days commemorate the dramatic events of our Faith and there are stories attached to each one of them. If we parents have told our toddlers even briefly about the Central Figures, they will understand at least something of what is going on during the devotional part of our celebrations. Some are joyful and some are sober. They should learn that there are sad and solemn occasions in the Bahá'í year, and that the commemorations will be arranged accordingly. As for Riḍván, Bahá'u'lláh bids His followers rejoice on that Day 'with exceeding gladness'[6] and describes it as 'the Day of supreme felicity'.[7] His utterances about its significance have been listed by Shoghi Effendi[8] and the cumulative effect is quite overpowering.

In a family where only one parent is a Bahá'í, the community should give particular attention to how it can help. As has been said, some non-Bahá'í spouses are very sympathetic, but some are not and the Bahá'ís concerned can have a very difficult time. They need all the spiritual and moral support the community can give and a mature and sympathetic handling of the situation. Concern on the part of the assembly for the spiritual and material welfare of every member of the community, including the children, will go a long way towards ensuring that 'firmly-grounded, busy and happy community life' which the Universal House of Justice says is 'envisioned when Local Spiritual Assemblies are truly effective'.[9]

Parents should also make sure that they avail themselves of their right to withdraw children from school on Holy Days. The best way to do this is to go and see the Head when the child is admitted to the school, explain that one is a Bahá'í and that there are certain days in the year which are Holy Days and on which one wishes the child or children to be withdrawn from school. If one goes with a list to give to the Head and explains that some of the days will fall at the weekend or during the school holidays anyway, and, of course, if there were an important event on that date, such as an examination, they would attend normally, the Head will usually be quite happy about it. To withdraw the children on Holy Days makes the point, not only to the Head but to the class teacher and the other children, that one's Faith is important. It may well provoke questions and stimulate interest. The children may be asked to tell the class something about the Faith, and young children, especially, are good at teaching the Faith because they haven't yet developed the inhibitions which they can have when they are older. I remember one little girl of about seven who went to school on April 20th and the class teacher remarked on her shining face. 'You're looking very happy today, Jane,' she said. 'Is it a special day today?' The child replied, 'I'm happy because it's Riḍván tomorrow.' Naturally this led to interested questions and Jane was delighted that she had been able to tell the class about the Faith.

Isolated believers

Although this section is written mainly with the isolated believers in mind, some of what follows, at least, can apply equally well to Bahá'ís living in communities; so I hope the latter will not just skip this section because they think it does not concern them. I have a particular love for the isolated friends and a great feeling for their situation, which is often very difficult, whether they be genuinely isolated or in a pioneer position before a community begins to develop round them.

When we do not have the example of other devoted Bahá'ís to set before our children, from whom they will absorb an attitude to worship as well as (we hope) from ourselves, it is doubly important to remember what Bahá'u'lláh says our attitude should be:

> They who are the beloved of God, in whatever place they gather and whomsoever they may meet, must evince, in their attitude towards God, and in the manner of their celebration of His praise and glory, such humility and submissiveness that every atom of the dust beneath their feet may attest the depth of their devotion.[10]

I would urge all isolated believers to be firm in their observances of the festivals of our Faith. You can, of course, go to neighbouring communities if they are handy, but I am more concerned here with those friends for whom this is not possible. Certainly, some forward planning is required, but you have to do this in other spheres of life, so there is no reason why it cannot be done in this; and there is nothing like having to search for prayers and suitable readings for making you familiar with your own Scriptures!

One of the great things about the Faith is that we can 'go to worship' together; we do not just send the children to Sunday School in order to get them out of the way while we watch the television – which is the best way to ensure that, as soon as they are old enough, they will abandon the religion that meant so little to their parents and do exactly the same thing. As was said in the first chapter, the Bahá'í Faith is for all of us: we are all subject to its demands, regardless of how old we are.

If you are isolated, your task is harder in that you have no community round you to give you moral support and spiritual encouragement. The challenge is much greater. However, it does have one advantage, in that you can arrange the Feasts and Holy Days in your own home to be held at a time and in a manner convenient to yourselves.

The Nineteen Day Feast

Although, as isolated believers, you cannot hold a full Feast, it should most certainly be held. You should not take the line that because you aren't a local spiritual assembly you can't hold it. While it is true that the Feast is an element of the Administration, it is not basically administrative in character. If we see it only as this, our Feast is not likely to be very inspiring; whereas 'Abdu'l-Bahá stresses over and over again the spiritual nature of the Feast:

... this fellowship is of the enjoyment of God, for the partaking of spiritual food, for the elucidation of spiritual subjects, for the discussion and interpretation of the teachings and counsels of God. It is absolute spirituality.[11]

As to the Nineteen Day Feast, it rejoiceth mind and heart. If this Feast be held in the proper fashion, the friends will, once in nineteen days, find themselves spiritually restored, and endued with a power that is not of this world.[12]

As has been said, it may be harder to celebrate the Feast on our own than when we are in a community, and this for a number of reasons. In the first place, we have actually to remember the dates (need for diary and dates filled in in advance!); we need a greater degree of self-discipline, because we have to prepare everything ourselves every time; our sense of commitment has to be stronger, perhaps, to see the need for observing it anyway. A comparison might be helpful:

Because we are alone, it doesn't mean we can manage without the regular spiritual sustenance which apparently is necessary when we live in a community; and Bahá'u'lláh has been very kind to us! In ratifying the Feast inaugurated by the Báb to be held but once in nineteen days, He evidently thinks that this is enough. Perhaps He expects the spiritual power generated on this occasion, and our own spiritual capacity and maturity, to be strong enough to last for this length of time before it has to be replenished. Whatever His reason, it is not much to ask that we make an effort once in what amounts to nearly three weeks, when we remember that Christians are expected to go to church once every seven days!

The spiritual power generated at a Feast is another reason for celebrating the Feast in our own area, even if we are totally alone. It will surely waft over the whole area, diffusing the divine fragrances in places we have no knowledge of, until one day it stirs the heart of some seeker who will bring us untold joy by wanting to hear about the Faith. What delight it is, too, when a member of a nearby community, as part of the local assembly's policy, comes to share *our* Feast with *us*; for as the Master says, '. . . where many are gathered together their force is greater'.[13] Two aren't exactly many, but the principle is the same: the spiritual force of two must be greater than that of one!

Indeed, when we are alone, in some ways it is even more important that we celebrate the Holy Days and Feasts, because when we are on our own it is very easy to become lax in our obligations; and when one becomes lax, it is more likely that one will become inactive. This is particularly true of the obligatory prayers. Somebody once said to me, putting into words what she suspected was the root cause of the increasing inactivity of a mutual friend, 'You know, if you don't say your obligatory prayer, your faith just goes.' I am sure she was right. I am sure, also, that the observance of the Feasts and Holy Days when we are isolated is a great help in maintaining a healthy spiritual life. It also establishes good habits and prepares both us and our children to take full part in community life in the future, when either we move to an area where a community already exists, or we ourselves become a goal and a community grows up round us.

One practical suggestion as to what you can do, especially if father doesn't come home until six or seven o'clock, is to hold two Feasts, one for the children combined with their tea and one later for yourselves. This will largely devolve upon mother, of course. When the children come home from school, they should wash and change into clean clothes (best ones, if they have such outfits), mother having first done so herself. They should enter the room where the Feast is being held clean and tidy, remembering that Bahá'u'lláh liked to see everyone 'well-groomed, and as neatly dressed as possible'[14] and that 'Abdu'l-Bahá said that although external cleanliness is only a physical thing it has a great effect on spirituality.[15] For the same reason, it goes without saying that the room should also be made to look nice. The prayers and readings should be chosen to suit the children's understanding, their various reading skills and their ability to concentrate. During the consultation period, you can obey 'Abdu'l-Bahá's wishes and 'elucidate spiritual subjects'[16] (answer their questions) and 'discuss and interpret the teachings and counsels of God'[17] (explain everything you think they may not have understood). Then there may be a Children's Feast Letter or a communication from the National

Spiritual Assembly to read with them, according to their age group. You can share any teaching plans you may have locally or in your goal area, and ask them to suggest ways in which they might help. They will be eager to tell you of any teaching they have done, especially at school. When this part of the Feast is over they can have their tea, for which you have prepared something a little extra, to make the occasion more festive. They should learn the names and dates of all the Feasts and look forward with pleasant anticipation to their regular occurrence.

Holy Days

Holy Days such as Naw-Rúz should be even more festive. In the first place, fathers (and mothers too if they have a job) should try to exercise their right not to go to work on these days, as well as taking the children out of school (if you are going to have the children at home, of course at least one of you will have to be off!). But it shouldn't end there. Holy Days are not intended as heaven-sent opportunities to catch up on homework, jobs about the house, or the mending. A certain amount has to be done in the way of preparing meals and washing up, but it should be possible to arrange the domestic chores in such a way that everybody is free to make this Holy Day a really family affair, having the devotional part and anything else you have planned, together.

Naw-Rúz and Riḍván, particularly, lend themselves to spring happiness. Why not fill the house with flowers? A trip to the country the day before to find pussy-willow, primroses, bluebells and other early flowers can be a most enjoyable outing. If you cannot do this, you may have some in the garden, or you can buy some. You can also make a Garden of Riḍván on a waterproof tray. The fact that you cannot visualise *exactly* what it must have been like doesn't matter; the description we have of it is sufficiently vivid for you to make a passable representation of it: avenues (not necessarily straight) lined with flower beds containing attempts at miniature rose bushes. Small sprouting twigs can be used for trees and suitable tiny clusters of flowers for rose bushes (or you can probably buy lots of little plastic rose bushes in your local toy shop). A strip of silver paper can be used to represent the River Tigris and soil or sand and moss for the flower beds and the river bank; and, depending on the colour of your tray, you can either leave it bare where the avenues are or use strips of brownish or sandy-coloured paper for this purpose. There must have been an open space where the tents were pitched, so you can put some more sand here, or something to look like grass. The tents can be constructed out of small, very thin strips of wood with some thin material over them. We know that Bahá'u'lláh rented three gardens but you may feel this is too much for one tray. If you think of your garden as the one Bahá'u'lláh chose for Himself, you will not, of course, try to make a model of Him, but you could pretend He was inside the tent and place a number of little figures nearby, with some waiting to go into His presence. If you keep the garden watered it will last all through the twelve days, and any flowers that do wilt can be replaced. Indeed, if you use your imagination, you can think up all sorts of ideas like this to make the Holy Days meaningful to your children. They will serve the dual purpose of helping the observances of Bahá'í life to become deeply implanted in the consciousness and also of teaching the Faith. People are bound to ask, 'What's that for?' and 'Why all the cards and flowers?' If the children take part in these preparations it will make them happy and they will associate the pattern of Bahá'í life with the creation of beautiful things. We can do all this when we live in a community too, of course, but here I am concerned with making the festivals of the Faith significant when the family is isolated. Such efforts confirm and strengthen our own faith as well as that of our children. They help all of us to feel some of that elation associated by 'Abdu'l-Bahá with the Spiritual Spring:

Do ye know in what cycle ye are created and in what age ye exist? This is the age of the Blessed Perfection and this is the time of the Greatest Name! This is the century of the Manifestation, the age of the Sun of the Horizons and the beautiful springtime of His Holiness the Eternal One!

The earth is in motion and growth; the mountains, hills and prairies are green and pleasant; the bounty is overflowing; the mercy universal; the rain is descending from the cloud of mercy; the brilliant Sun is shining; the full moon is ornamenting the horizon of ether; the great ocean-tide is flooding every little stream; the gifts are successive; the favors consecutive; and the refreshing breeze is blowing, wafting the fragrant perfume of the blossoms. Boundless treasure is in the hand of the King of Kings! Lift the hem of thy garment in order to receive it.

If we are not happy and joyous at this season, for what other season shall we wait and for what other time shall we look?

This is the time for growing; the season for joyous gathering! Take the cup of the Testament in thy hand; leap and dance with ecstasy in the triumphal procession of the Covenant! Lay your confidence in the everlasting bounty, turn to the presence of the generous God; ask assistance from the Kingdom of Abhá; seek confirmation from the Supreme World; turn thy vision to the horizon of eternal wealth; and pray for help from the Source of Mercy!

Soon shall ye see the friends attaining their longed-for destination and pitching their tents, while we are but in the first day of our journey.

This period of time is the Promised Age, the assembling of the human race to the 'Resurrection Day' and now is the great 'Day of Judgment.' Soon the whole world, as in springtime, will change its garb. The turning and falling of the autumn leaves is past; the bleakness of the winter time is over. The new year hath appeared and the spiritual springtime is at hand. The black earth is becoming a verdant garden; the deserts and mountains are teeming with red flowers; from the borders of the wilderness the tall grasses are standing like advance guards before the cypress and jessamine trees; while the birds are singing among the rose branches like the angels in the highest heavens, announcing the glad-tidings of the approach of that spiritual spring, and the sweet music of their voices is causing the real essence of all things to move and quiver.[18]

Christmas

Quite apart from anything else, we have to remember that Riḍván, say, has to compete with the Christian festival of Christmas in our children's minds. Christmas can be a very wonderful occasion and unless we make an effort to ensure that Riḍván or the Birth of Bahá'u'lláh are also very wonderful occasions, our children will grow up still feeling that Christmas is more important. We have to bear in mind, however, that our anniversaries are first and foremost *Holy* Days, and not allow them to degenerate into the kind of commercial bonanza that is now associated, most regrettably, with the birth of Christ. We know the Guardian advised that, amongst themselves, the Bahá'ís should not celebrate Christmas,[19] but we may feel that there are some circumstances where, for the sake of the children – and of course if one parent is a Christian – we should celebrate it. In this case, I think we should guard against remembering the decorations, the food and the presents and forgetting the reason why we have them. This, too, is a Holy Day and I think it is fitting that we include a short devotional period in our celebrations, with readings and prayers from both the Christian and Bahá'í Scriptures, so that neither we nor our children lose sight of this fact.

The whole question of Christmas looms so large in the consciousness of small children living in Christian countries that it may be useful to go into it in more detail. Father Christmas, carols, Christmas trees, decorations, presents, turkey, plum pudding, Christmas cakes, all the fairyland of tinsel and glitter, the magic of Christmas Eve, the excitement of Christmas Day itself, going on all around them and building up for weeks beforehand until the climax finally comes – how *can* we expect them not to want to share in its delights? As has been said, each couple must decide for themselves how much of it they are going to introduce into their own situation; but where they decide that it must be nil, they will have to be very, very careful how they handle it.

If, for instance, your child of three or four asks when Father Christmas is going to bring him/her presents, the answer must not be negative. A happy outcome will repay some time spent on reading up the life of the original Santa Claus – Saint Nicholas – and thinking about how you are going to answer the question, *before it is asked*, so that you are not taken off your guard and rendered speechless. Having said, 'Come, I will tell you a story', you will take the child on your knee and, starting as all good stories start, with 'Once upon a time . . .', you will tell him/her about Saint Nicholas (leaving out the gory bits), and then proceed something like this: 'So you see, Santa Claus loved children and wanted to be kind to them. He loved Jesus – you remember about Jesus, don't you? . . . Yes, that's right. Well, Jesus said we should be kind to children, too. People who loved Jesus thought it would be nice to have a special day when they could remember Santa Claus. They thought about Santa Claus and they thought about Jesus. They remembered Christmas was Jesus' birthday and so they began to give children presents about that time, in memory of Saint Nicholas. In those days, though, the presents were only for *good* children – you're good, aren't you? Yes, of course you are! Well, Santa Claus couldn't be everywhere at once, so the story grew up that he came down the chimney in the middle of the night when the children were in bed and asleep, so they couldn't see him. But then there had to be a great big fireplace for him to come out of; and we haven't got any fireplaces in our bedrooms, have we? So he couldn't do that, could he? Bahá'u'lláh loved children too and *He* told everyone to be kind to each other; but He said we should give presents and have parties during the Intercalary Days and that's what we Bahá'ís do. It's only two months after Christmas, so you haven't long to wait to get Mummy and Daddy's present, have you? So if Father Christmas can't get to your room because you haven't got a fireplace, it doesn't matter, does it? You'll get some presents later. And just think! You will get some presents when (mention the names of some little friends) won't! And you can give them some then, too. Won't that be exciting?'

If, on your shopping expeditions, you find Santa Claus giving out gifts in every other store, it should sooner or later dawn on your child that there is something a little odd here. How *can* there be so many Santa Clauses? You've only just seen one two minutes ago. It *can't* be the same one – there hasn't been time! The child may work it out for himself that this cannot be the real Santa Claus; and if this one isn't the real Santa Claus, what about the one that is supposed to come down chimneys? Perhaps that's not true, either. So where *do* the presents come from? When he eventually learns that it is the children's own Mummies and Daddies who put the presents in the stockings, you can point out that there isn't much difference between putting presents in stockings and giving them at the Intercalary Days.

The likelihood is that most of their relations and friends

are not Bahá'ís and will be sending them presents anyway; and when they are old enough they will reciprocate. We don't become totally negative about it because our celebrations are different. The same must be true of the festivals of other Faiths. I have not experienced them so I cannot make suggestions as to what can be done; but if parents of Muslim or Hindu background, say, understand the principle of what has been said, I am sure it can be applied in a comparable situation.

Intercalary Days

One of the things I have always liked about our period of 'hospitality and the giving of gifts' – Ayyám-i-Há, the Intercalary Days – is that they are not associated with a Holy Day and so, it is to be hoped, our Holy Days will *not* follow the fate of Christmas. This is our special period set aside by the Founder of our Faith, when we can be generous and hospitable. We should be both these things anyway but something extra can be done during this period. Having parties during the Intercalary Days, to which you invite your neighbours and friends, is a good way of introducing the Faith to new people; they will wonder why you are having a party at such an unusual time of year and this gives you a good opportunity to explain why. It is my personal hope that this period will gradually supersede the times of present-giving associated with Christmas and Naw-Rúz. If Bahá'ís of Christian background have had to give up celebrating Christmas, perhaps it is not too much to hope that those whose background emphasises Naw-Rúz as the time for presents, will gradually feel able to dispense with this traditional custom and both adopt a new pattern in their lives. Many years ago we had some Hindu friends in the town where we lived. One Christmas, they sent us a card and so we sent them one. We thus had the slightly ridiculous situation of Hindus and Bahá'ís exchanging greetings for a Holy Day which neither of them celebrated (but it shows the power of Christmas!). More recently, we received a present from a neighbour one Christmas, quite unexpectedly. There was no time to respond in like kind and we didn't want it to look as though we had forgotten. So we thanked the lady and returned the compliment during the Intercalary Days; and this has now become the annual custom.

To those who may object that all this is still very materialistic, let me say again that we should try to make our Holy Days truly spiritual occasions; and with the new dimension of social and economic development we should give more thought to 'Abdu'l-Bahá's exhortation to initiate humanitarian projects on Holy Days. This is fine for us grown-ups, but the material side of Christmas is very important to children and we shall not ween them away from it by clamping down on it and telling them that they must be spiritual. Small children do not understand this concept – and neither do a lot of grown-ups, for that matter. It seems to me that the better way is to concentrate on our own period of 'hospitality and the giving of gifts', which, as has been said, is not associated with any Holy Day. We have to teach our children to 'be generous in prosperity and thankful in adversity'[20] and that 'it is more blessed to give than to receive'.[21] We must not, in our enthusiasm for spirituality, stifle the generous impulses that well up at these times. A well-chosen present lifts the heart and also cheers the one who spends time looking for the 'exactly right' gift to give to a much-loved relation or friend. In my childhood, my brothers and I made all our presents and so, later, did my own children – and a lot of fun we all had doing it. I remember, one autumn, starting to make a lace-edged tray cloth for my grandmother, the idea being that, if I worked at it a little at a time, it would be ready in time for Christmas; and my wise and imaginative mother made me start sewing the lace on down the long side, so that by the time I was really getting tired of it, there was only the short side left to do.

So to return to the necessity of celebrating the festivals of our Faith, whether we are in a community or on our own; when we remember that Bahá'u'lláh tells us that our 'whole duty . . . in this Day is to attain that share of the flood of grace which God poureth forth' for us[22] – and that one very effective way of obtaining some of our share of this flood of grace is at the Nineteen Day Feasts and Holy Days; and when we call to mind His words, 'The Word of God hath set the heart of the world afire; how regrettable if ye fail to be enkindled with its flame!';[23] why then we shall surely all ardently wish to commemorate all the festivals associated with our Best-Beloved, in this, His new attire!

7

Tests

God and suffering

We now come to the last – but by far the most important – aspect of our training, namely, the acceptance of the Will of God.

In this connection I believe two things are essential in our training of our children: an adequate conception of God and an understanding of the reasons for sacrifice and suffering. If one talks to people who are bitter about religion, one often finds that these two things are lacking. They have a rather infantile, anthropomorphic conception of God and a belief that the answer to prayer should always be 'yes' or there is no God. Also, they don't understand why they (or other people) should suffer when they have done nothing to deserve it. As far as tests and difficulties are concerned, we have to bring our children to a recognition of the fact that, ultimately, God doeth whatsoever He willeth and He shall not be asked of His doings. 'Abdu'l-Bahá tells us that

> The souls who bear the tests of God become the manifestations of great bounties; for the divine trials cause some souls to become entirely lifeless, while they cause the holy souls to ascend to the highest degree of love and firmness. They cause progress and they also cause retrogression.[1]

Bahá'u'lláh's statement that 'God will never deal unjustly with anyone, neither will He test a soul beyond its power'[2] is true for the one whose faith is strong. Retrogression is caused when we think we can pull ourselves up by our own shoe-strings and manage without His help.

All around us we see a rising tide of suffering: marriages break up, families are disrupted, children become deprived and maladjusted – and child abuse is on the increase. This is partly helped on by either the romantic and slushy rubbish on the one hand, or the downright immoral sex and violence on the other, which are churned out all the time in magazines, popular novels and on the television. The one gives the impression that marriage and family life are an unending bed of roses without any kind of strain or tension; the other plays on people's human lusts, selfishness, greed and egotism, to the extent that extra-marital relations are portrayed as normal and 'emancipated' and perfectly acceptable in the modern world, and aggressiveness a virtue.

One of the greatest contributory factors in this depressing state of affairs is, I think, what might appear to be the growing inability of people to face up to difficulties. They rush to pills for almost any little ache, whether it be tummy-ache, heart-ache or toe-ache. Tranquillisers are consumed by the ton. From what one reads and hears, one might perhaps be forgiven for thinking that the ability of people in general to stand up to pain or suffering of any description becomes less and less. Difficulties are a test of faith and through them our souls grow and develop. In time of trouble we need to enter the intensive prayer unit and God will nurse us through.

So let us teach our children to accept difficulty as a gift from God – a gift for which they should be grateful, because it gives them a chance to show what they are made of; and let us set the example when we ourselves are faced with it. I don't mean the stiff-upper-lip mentality: let us acknowledge our humanity and have a good cry if we feel like it – men as well as women. It's a safety valve which God has given us and should not be despised as 'weakness'; but 'Abdu'l-Bahá says:

> . . . all our sorrow, pain, shame and grief, are born in the world of matter; whereas the spiritual Kingdom never causes sadness. A man living with his thoughts in this Kingdom knows perpetual joy. The ills all flesh is heir to do not pass him by, but they only touch the surface of his life, the depths are calm and serene.[3]

Just as to teach is the epitome of service, so the epitome of faith is to be able to say with Job, 'Though He slay me, yet will I trust in Him.'[4]

We must try to help our children to arrive at the kind of steadfastness referred to by Bahá'u'lláh in the following passage:

> . . . to remain steadfast in the Cause of God – exalted be His glory – and to be unswerving in His love. And this can in no wise be attained except through full recognition of Him; and full recognition cannot be obtained save by faith in the blessed words: 'He doeth whatsoever He willeth.' Whoso tenaciously cleaveth unto this sublime word and drinketh deep from the living waters of utterance which are inherent therein, will be imbued with such a constancy that all the books of the world will be powerless to deter him from the Mother Book. O how glorious is this sublime station, this exalted rank, this ultimate purpose![5]

If we can instil this in a right way into our children's consciousness from their earliest years, we shall have gone a long way towards helping them to stand up to tests later.

We should teach our children to be happy with the will of God, whether He seems to answer their prayers or no. There is a delightful story of a little girl who wanted blue eyes. She had a lovely pair of brown ones but thought she would prefer to have them blue. She told her mother at bedtime that she was going to pray for blue eyes. Her mother considered herself an atheist and poured scorn on the idea. However, the little girl was not to be put off and insisted that she was going to pray for blue eyes. So she did. Next morning she came down to breakfast with the same pair of lovely brown eyes as usual and her mother said, 'There you are, I told you nothing would happen. God didn't answer your prayers.' The little girl replied, 'Oh yes, He did! He said "No!"'

This child had more understanding and sense than her mother. One could point out that here was a perfect example of the irrational attitude of an atheist who, while denying the existence of God, yet half expected a miracle to be performed, and when it wasn't, was confirmed in her scepticism – as if such a totally impossible thing were enough on which to base belief in God! This child, whose faith was pure and strong, was more realistic; and because she was more realistic, she was able to accept without question the negative answer to her prayer. Our children have to understand, like this little girl, that God *always* answers prayers – but that He does sometimes say 'No'.

The pull of the outside world

When our children begin to grow up, and especially during their adolescence, they will feel the pull of the outside world – and it can be a very glittering, attractive pull. When they finally leave home to study or to work, they are surrounded by an alien and largely unsympathetic community. Whatever we may have taught them, they will find themselves severely tested. However much they may know in their minds that they must obey Bahá'u'lláh's laws and observe certain standards, the temptation to follow the crowd is tremendous, especially when we remember that they may not yet have acquired true faith in Bahá'u'lláh and therefore a real understanding and acceptance of His laws. They need at least to have developed a lively conscience by then. It is interesting to note that Bahá'u'lláh links this with the fear of God:

> Verily I say: The fear of God hath ever been a sure defence and a safe stronghold for all the peoples of the world. It is the chief cause of the protection of mankind, and the supreme instrument for its preservation. Indeed, there existeth in man a faculty which deterreth him from, and guardeth him against, whatever is unworthy and unseemly, and which is known as his sense of shame.[6]

Our aim, we must bear in mind, 'is to create a society which in turn will react on the character of the individual'.[7] This means Divine civilisation, and this, 'Abdu'l-Bahá tells us,

> so traineth every member of society that no one, with the exception of a negligible few, will undertake to commit a crime. There is thus a great difference between the prevention of crime through measures that are violent and retaliatory, and so training the people, and enlightening them, and spiritualizing them, that without any fear of punishment or vengeance to come, they will shun all criminal acts. They will, indeed, look upon the very commission of a crime as a great disgrace and in itself the harshest of punishments.[8]

This cannot be achieved without the development of conscience and its concomitant, a sense of shame. The lack of them may well be the cause of a lot of behaviour which distresses us in the world today, in view of what Bahá'u'lláh says about the sense of shame:

> This, however, is confined to but a few; all have not possessed and do not possess it.[9]

Let us make sure that all we Bahá'ís are amongst those few who do possess this faculty and can recognise evil, or even just godlessness, when we meet it. If we do make a mistake, let us readily admit it and say, 'I'm sorry – it was my fault', and not try to justify our actions by blaming someone else. 'Passing the buck' is not one of the virtues listed by Bahá'u'lláh, either for individuals or for divine institutions! 'Abdu'l-Bahá says:

> Children must be most carefully watched over, protected and trained; in such consisteth true parenthood and parental mercy.
> Otherwise, the children will turn into weeds growing wild, and become the cursed, Infernal Tree,* knowing not right from wrong, distinguishing not the highest of human qualities from all that is mean and vile; they will be brought up in vainglory, and will be hated of the Forgiving Lord.
> Wherefore doth every child, new-risen in the garden of Heavenly love, require the utmost training and care.[10]

It is particularly important to remember, where the education of Bahá'í children is concerned, that the Word of God is the unerring Balance in which all else is weighed,[11] because they will come up against all sorts of ideas in their schools and colleges that run counter to what Bahá'u'lláh teaches; ideas which exert a subtle – and sometimes pernicious – influence in the wrong direction, and which are put over with such authority that the one-on-his-own, who has yet to acquire faith for himself, may very well question whether or not Bahá'u'lláh is right. For instance, some literature which is considered suitable for older pupils to study might well come under the heading of

> . . . materialistic works that are current among those who see only natural causation, and tales of love, and books that arouse the passions[12]

* The Zaqqúm. *Qur'án* 37: 60, 44: 43.

which 'Abdu'l-Bahá says should not be read in schools. I am not suggesting that Bahá'í young people should refuse to read the books they are given. Obviously, they must study what is set. The point I am making is that they must have a yardstick by which to measure the worth of what they study. They must *know* that the unerring Balance is the Word of God; they must have the courage to state, if necessary, that even if it takes the scientists a thousand years to come round to proving independently that what Bahá'u'lláh says is true, they *will* eventually do so. Without being aggressive about it, they must be prepared to say that this is what our teachings state to be the case, however much science, in its present stage of development, may 'prove' to the contrary. They must also have the strength of character to refrain from joining in actions which they know to be wrong. This is an aspect of faith. You really have got to believe that Bahá'u'lláh is right; but when you do, nothing will shake you, no matter what the world may say or do:

. . . be thou so steadfast in My love that thy heart shall not waver, even if the swords of the enemies rain blows upon thee and all the heavens and the earth arise against thee.[13]

It should be our aim as parents so to train the next generation that they will acquire this kind of faith for themselves.

Let us not underestimate the pernicious and subtle influences with which our children are surrounded. They are so young and so vulnerable! It requires courage to stand out and be different when all their friends are doing the opposite to what they have been taught – and apparently getting away with it. They, who are not yet convinced, may not see why they should not do the same things, since no adverse effects seem to follow. When one is young and bursting with an abundance of physical life and energy, eternity is a long way off and the things of the spirit often unreal. Faith, the ultimate sanction behind any law, has yet to be acquired; and while it is true that in the time of testing they are more likely to acquire it, their only safeguard before that happens may well be their willpower, their self-respect and their sense of shame.

Freedom is a condition which is prized above almost everything else today, whereas submission and obedience are considered dead virtues. Freedom, in many – perhaps one could say most – young people's minds means doing what you like all the time; though, regretfully, freedom of an equal kind is not always allowed by these same young people to others whose ideas differ from their own. In discarding the restraints imposed by their parents or society as a whole, they merely throw away one set of rules in favour of another; and whereas the rules they throw overboard did at least have the sanction of a generally accepted code of morals behind them, so that everybody knew what was right and what was wrong (even if not everybody lived up to it), the ones they take on have no sanction at all beyond egotism and being 'with it'. This has had so much effect even on older people that one often hears someone say, 'Perhaps I'm old-fashioned, but . . .' We have to be clear that right and wrong are not fashions, like clothes, to be cast aside next season in favour of something more *à la mode*. Standards of right and wrong *are* standards and some of them are eternal. It may seem a paradox to the young that if you want to be free you must submit. Christ said, 'If ye continue in my word, then are ye my disciples indeed. And ye shall know the truth and the truth shall make you free.'[14] Bahá'u'lláh reiterates this and explains further that true freedom means submitting to the Will of God:

Consider the pettiness of men's minds. They ask for that

which injureth them, and cast away the thing that profiteth them. They are, indeed, of those that are far astray. We find some men desiring liberty, and priding themselves therein. Such men are in the depths of ignorance . . .

Regard men as a flock of sheep that need a shepherd for their protection. This, verily, is the truth, the certain truth. We approve of liberty in certain circumstances, and refuse to sanction it in others. We, verily, are the All-Knowing.

Say: True liberty consisteth in man's submission unto My commandments, little as ye know it. Were men to observe that which We have sent down unto them from the Heaven of Revelation, they would, of a certainty, attain unto perfect liberty. Happy is the man that hath apprehended the Purpose of God in whatever He hath revealed from the Heaven of His Will, that pervadeth all created things. Say: The liberty that profiteth you is to be found nowhere except in complete servitude unto God, the Eternal Truth. Whoso hath tasted of its sweetness will refuse to barter it for all the dominion of earth and heaven.[15]

Being 'with it' is a chimera. It is also a morass: it has no solid foundation. This so-called freedom is the essence of selfishness and its ultimate and logical conclusion is anarchy.

Bahá'u'lláh, in the middle of the passage just quoted, says:

Liberty must, in the end, lead to sedition, whose flames none can quench. Thus warneth you He Who is the Reckoner, the All-Knowing. Know ye that the embodiment of liberty and its symbol is the animal. That which beseemeth man is submission unto such restraints as will protect him from his own ignorance, and guard him against the harm of the mischief-maker. Liberty causeth man to overstep the bounds of propriety, and to infringe on the dignity of his station. It debaseth him to the level of extreme depravity and wickedness.[16]

'Abdu'l-Bahá tells us that the very commission of a crime should be sufficient punishment in itself. Conversely, the fact of having done a right action, especially in the face of a challenging choice, brings its reward. To feel right with God – what Christians call 'a state of grace' – is the most wonderful and satisfying of rewards. Children can feel this, if they have been properly taught, but a little human encouragement may be necessary to help them to reach the state where they can dispense with material reward. Both reward and punishment should be administered sparingly. The child can find out for himself that it feels dreadful to have done something wrong; on the other hand, the good pleasure of his parents when he has done something right and good is enough for a young child. We should guard against ourselves corrupting our own children by anything that might be considered bribery!

One morning, young Robert's mother found a piece of paper on the kitchen table after he had gone out to play. On it Robert had written:

For running errands	20p
For washing up	10p
For feeding the hens	5p
For sweeping the yard	20p
For fetching your prescription	10p
Total	65p

She read this through with a feeling of sadness and then made out a similar one for Robert to find when he came home:

For getting your meals	—
For doing your washing	—
For mending your clothes	—
For cleaning your room	—
For helping you with your homework	—
Total	—

Robert learned a lot about love that day.

The smallness of our numbers at present makes it even more difficult for our children to obey Bahá'u'lláh. They may be the only ones in their school and later college or place of work who don't do this or that, and on the whole children and young people don't like to feel 'out of it'. They may, like the ugly duckling, be going to turn into beautiful swans, but in the meantime the going can be very difficult. For this reason it is extremely important that we, their parents, visit Bahá'í friends with them, especially where there are children, and receive visits in return; that we take them to weekend schools and summer schools, etc., where they will mingle with others of like mind and with the same code of behaviour, to give them moral support.

A spiritual Everest

We need to teach our children that it is exciting to obey laws and much more fun to try to be good than simply to jolly along with the crowd – that amorphous mass where 'effort' is an unknown word. There is very little left in the physical world for man to conquer or to satisfy his need for adventure – and we can't all go rushing off to the moon; but there *is* still a challenge in life and we do still have a battle on; perhaps a harder struggle, for most of us, even than climbing Mount Everest. We have to conquer that most treacherous mountain of all, the one called Ego. Nobody can start too soon, so it is essential that we point the way up the lower slopes to our children from the day they are born. We cannot start too soon, but neither must we expect to conquer it in one concerted onslaught. We are not offered instant perfection when we sign the declaration card. The answer to this dilemma is given by Colby Ives. He once asked 'Abdu'l-Bahá how it could ever be possible for me, deep in the mass of weak and selfish humanity, ever to hope to attain when the goal was so high and great. He said that it is to be accomplished little by little; little by little. And I thought to myself, I have all eternity for this journey from self to God. The thing to do is to get started.[17]

It is during the period covered by the term 'Bahá'í Youth' that the value of developing spiritual habits will stand them in good stead, especially that of prayer. The purpose of all tests is to bring the soul nearer to God and this cannot be achieved without them. 'Abdu'l-Bahá says:

> The mind and spirit of man advance when he is tried by suffering. The more the ground is ploughed the better the seed will grow, the better the harvest will be. Just as the plough furrows the earth deeply, purifying it of weeds and thistles, so suffering and tribulation free man from the petty affairs of this worldly life until he arrives at a state of complete detachment. His attitude in this world will be that of divine happiness. Man is, so to speak, unripe: the heat of the fire of suffering will mature him. Look back to the times past and you will find that the greatest men have suffered most.[18]

Unfortunately, it seems to be a fact that men cannot make progress without suffering of some kind. If we want to develop certain qualities, such as courage, patience, love, mercy, kindness and so on, we cannot expect to be given these qualities on a plate. What happens is that we find ourselves in situations – no doubt God-given – where we can learn to develop these qualities. If we will not learn by being told, we have to find out by experience; and if we will not learn our lesson the first time, it will be repeated until we do:

> By refusing to get the spiritual value from the tests which come to us we leave ourselves open to the same test recurring with greater severity, and we have thereby increased our

difficulties instead of decreasing them. God is thorough and perfect in all things, and man is not through with any problem until he has mastered it.

'Abdu'l-Bahá, in answer to a question put to Him on this subject by a pilgrim visiting Him in 1915, replied in the following words: 'The same test comes again in greater degree, until it is shown that a former weakness has become a strength, and the power to overcome evil has been established . . .'[19]

So the next time we moan about how difficult the children are becoming, how irritating is that fellow in the office who whistles through his teeth all the time, or what a pest the neighbours' cat can be if you don't watch it, let us try to remember that we prayed for patience and forbearance and these situations are probably just what we need in answer to our prayer – for how can we develop patience and forbearance if we have nobody to practise them on?

We must do the best we can

We have to do the best we can: teach our children the best that we know; that service to the Cause of God is the greatest service they can render to humanity, and service to humanity their highest aspiration. At one time, you heard it said that you shouldn't teach your children the Faith because they had to be free, at fifteen, to make their own minds up. This is the most cruel form of deprivation and neglect that any parent can inflict upon a child! How can he choose what he knows nothing about? He will flounder and more often than not will either just drift through life or join something else. 'Abdu'l-Bahá is quite firm on the matter: parents

. . . must train their children with life and heart and teach them in the school of virtue and perfection. They must not be lax in this matter; they must not be inefficient.[20]

Apart from which, if we really believe ourselves that we

have found the Truth, how can we deny it to our own children? If *we* don't teach them, the outside world will; and if *we* don't give them a scale of values, they will imbibe one from the television.

However, in the end, every soul has its own path to tread. Those of us who are converts have found ours; our children must find what they have been brought up in. We must try to understand their need to do this; try to understand their problems in and with the Faith – because by the time they are in their late teens they will have them – and help them to understand the Faith. We should really be glad when this happens, because if the Faith is to mean anything to them, if it is to become part of them – as it must if they are to be able to render it worthwhile service – they must struggle and suffer. 'Do they think, when they say "We believe" that they will not be tested?'[21] When our young people say they aren't sure if they believe in Bahá'u'lláh and think it would be 'hypocritical' to continue calling themselves Bahá'ís, so they think they'd better resign, we have to be very understanding but also very clear in our guidance. The truth of the matter may well be that they haven't yet acquired *certitude* and because of this are succumbing to pressures from their peer group to break one or more of Bahá'u'lláh's laws. They may even say that they think they should know what these things are that they aren't supposed to indulge in. As one young man said to me recently, 'Well, I would say to them that this argument implies that these things are worth doing, whereas in fact they're not. Why should they want to waste their time on things that aren't worth doing in the first place?' It may be that your adolescent offspring doesn't want to break a law but is just uncertain and still thinks it would be hypocritical to go on being a Bahá'í. My advice to such young people has always been, '*Don't* leave the Faith. If you do, you will have no anchor for your life and you will, sooner or later, be influenced away from its standards because you will have no reason not to do what everybody else is doing. This is a passing phase, something you will work your way through if you try hard enough. If you move out of the influence of the Word of God, what else is there? It is better to stay in and try to sort yourself out *in*side the Faith; and pray. Pray for guidance. Pray like the man who said to Christ, "Lord, I believe. Help thou mine unbelief".'[22]

Christ said, 'Many are called but few are chosen.'[23] In order to be chosen – to become a channel for God's grace to man – our young people must suffer. They must pass through the fire of tests in order that the dross may be burned away and the pure, refined metal emerge. 'Abdu'l-Bahá says: 'It is the duty of parents to perfectly and thoroughly train their children.'[24] If we have taught them properly they will come through in the end; but it does require that the teaching should have been done. We may not feel that it has always been perfect; but at least it should have been thorough!

Conclusion

So, education in the Bahá'í family includes the parents as well as the children. We have only touched the surface of the subject. This education is in a school which continues throughout life. Perhaps we never graduate. The task is long and arduous, but we have the assurance that we are doing something which is leading to the creation of the Kingdom of God on earth.

O ye friends of God! Because, in this most momentous of ages, the Sun of Truth hath risen at the highest point of the spring equinox, and cast its rays on every clime, it shall kindle such tremulous excitement, it shall release such vibrations in the world of being, it shall stimulate such growth and development, it shall stream out with such a glory of light, and clouds of grace shall pour down such plentiful waters, and fields and plains shall teem with such a galaxy of sweet-smelling plants and blooms, that this lowly earth will become the Abhá Kingdom, and this nether world the world above. Then will this fleck of dust be as the vast circle of the skies, this human place the palace-court of God, this spot of clay the day-spring of the endless favours of the Lord of Lords.[25]

Epilogue

Fill Thou, O God, our home with harmony and happiness, with laughter and delight, with radiant kindliness and overflowing joy, that in the union of our hearts Thy love may find a lodging place, and Thou Thyself mayst make this home of ours Thine Own!

O God, make Thou this home of ours the garden of affection, a ripening place of love, where the hidden powers of our hearts may unfold, expand and bear the fruit of an abiding joy.

Unto Thee, O God, we dedicate this home. Cleanse it from all that is alien to Thee that it may become fit for Thine acceptance, and may be to friend and stranger as to ourselves a place of peace, a refuge from materialism, a herald of Thy Kingdom.[1]

George Townsend

Appendix

Letter from the Universal House of Justice, 28 December 1980

The House of Justice suggests that all statements in the Holy Writings concerning specific areas of the relationship between men and women should be considered in the light of the general principle of equality between the sexes that has been authoritatively and repeatedly enunciated in the Sacred Texts. In one of His Tablets 'Abdu'l-Bahá asserts: 'In this divine age the bounties of God have encompassed the world of women. Equality of men and women, except in some negligible instances, has been fully and categorically announced. Distinctions have been utterly removed.' That men and women differ from one another in certain characteristics and functions is an inescapable fact of nature; the important thing is that 'Abdu'l-Bahá regards such inequalities as remain between the sexes as being 'negligible'.

The relationship between husband and wife must be viewed in the context of the Bahá'í ideal of family life. Bahá'u'lláh came to bring unity to the world, and a fundamental unity is that of the family. Therefore, one must believe that the Faith is intended to strengthen the family, not weaken it, and one of the keys to the strengthening of unity is loving consultation. The atmosphere within a Bahá'í family as within the community as a whole should express 'the keynote of the Cause of God' which, the beloved Guardian has stated, 'is not dictatorial authority but humble fellowship, not arbitrary power, but the spirit of frank and loving consultation'.

A family, however, is a very special kind of 'community'. The Research Department has not come across any statements which specifically name the father as responsible for the 'security, progress and unity of the family' . . . but it can be inferred from a number of the responsibilities placed upon him, that the father can be regarded as the 'head' of the family. The members of a family all have duties and responsibilities towards one another and to the family as a whole, and these duties and responsibilities vary from member to member because of their natural relationships. The parents have the inescapable duty to educate their children – but not vice versa; the children have the duty to obey their parents – the parents do not obey the children; the mother – not the father – bears the children, nurses them in babyhood, and is thus their first educator, hence daughters have a prior right to education over sons and, as the Guardian's secretary has written on his behalf, 'The task of bringing up a Bahá'í child, as emphasized time and again in Bahá'í Writings, is the chief responsibility of the mother, whose unique privilege is indeed to create in her home such conditions as would be most conducive to both his material and spiritual welfare and advancement. The training which the child first receives through his mother constitutes the strongest foundation for his future development.' A corollary of this responsibility of the mother is her right to be supported by her husband – a husband has no explicit right to be supported by his wife. This principle of the husband's responsibility to provide for and protect the family can be seen applied also in the law of intestacy which provides that the family's dwelling place passes, on the father's death, not to his widow, but to his eldest son; the son at the same time has the responsibility to care for his mother.

It is in this context of mutual and complementary duties and responsibilities that one should read the Tablet in which 'Abdu'l-Bahá gives the following exhortation:

> O Handmaids of the Self-Sustaining Lord! Exert your efforts so that you may attain the honour and privilege ordained for women. Undoubtedly the greatest glory of women is servitude at His threshold and submissiveness at His door; it is the possession of a vigilant heart, and praise of the incomparable God; it is heartfelt love towards other handmaids and spotless chastity; it is obedience to and consideration for their husbands and the education and care of their children; and it is tranquillity, and dignity, perseverance in the remembrance of the Lord, and the utmost enkindlement and attraction.

This exhortation to the utmost degree of spirituality and self-abnegation should not be read as a legal definition giving the husband absolute authority over his wife, for, in a letter written to an individual believer on 22 July 1943, the beloved Guardian's secretary wrote on his behalf:

> The Guardian, in his remarks . . . about parents and children, wives' and husbands' relations in America, meant that there is a tendency in that country for children to be too independent of the wishes of their parents and lacking in the respect due to them. Also wives, in some cases, have a tendency to exert an unjust degree of domination over their husbands which, of course, is not right, any more than that the husband should unjustly dominate his wife.

In any group, however loving the consultation, there are nevertheless points on which, from time to time, agreement cannot be reached. In a Spiritual Assembly this dilemma is resolved by a majority vote. There can, however, be no majority where only two parties are involved, as in the case of a husband and wife. There are, therefore, times when a wife should defer to her husband, and times when a husband should defer to his wife, but neither should ever unjustly dominate the other. In short, the relationship between husband and wife should be as held forth in the prayer revealed by 'Abdu'l-Bahá which is often read at Bahá'í weddings: 'Verily they are married in obedience to Thy command. Cause them to become the signs of harmony and unity till the end of time.'

These are all relationships within the family, but there is a much wider sphere of relationships between men and women than in the home, and this too we should consider in the context of Bahá'í society, not in that of past or present social norms. For example, although the mother is the first educator of the child, and the most important formative influence in his development, the father also has the responsibility of educating his children, and this responsibility is so weighty that Bahá'u'lláh has stated that a father who fails to exercise it forfeits his rights of fatherhood. Similarly, although the primary responsibility for supporting the family financially is placed upon the husband, this does not by any means imply that the place of women is confined to the home. On the contrary, 'Abdu'l-Bahá has stated:

> In this Revelation of Bahá'u'lláh, the women go neck and neck with the men. In no movement will they be left behind. Their rights with men are equal in degree. They will enter all the administrative branches of politics. They will attain in all such a degree as will be considered the very highest station of the world of humanity and will take part in all affairs. (*Paris Talks*, p. 182)

and again:

> So it will come to pass that when women participate fully and equally in the affairs of the world, enter confidently and capably

the great arena of laws and politics, war will cease; . . . (*The Promulgation of Universal Peace*, Vol. II, p. 369)

In the Tablet of the World, Bahá'u'lláh Himself has envisaged that women as well as men would be breadwinners in stating:

> Everyone, whether man or woman, should hand over to a trusted person a portion of what he or she earneth through trade, agriculture or other occupation, for the training and education of children, to be spent for this purpose with the knowledge of the Trustees of the House of Justice. (*Tablets of Bahá'u'lláh*, p. 90)

A very important element in the attainment of such equality is Bahá'u'lláh's provision that boys and girls must follow essentially the same curriculum in schools.[1]

Key to References

ADJ	*The Advent of Divine Justice.* Shoghi Effendi. Wilmette, Bahá'í Publishing Trust, 1956.
BA	*Bahá'í Administration.* Letters from Shoghi Effendi. Wilmette, Bahá'í Publishing Trust, 1960.
BE	*Bahá'í Education: A Compilation.* Research Department of the Universal House of Justice. London: Bahá'í Publishing Trust, 1978.
BNE	*Bahá'u'lláh and the New Era.* J. E. Esslemont. Wilmette, Bahá'í Publishing Trust, 1980.
BP	*Bahá'í Prayers: A Selection.* London: Bahá'í Publishing Trust, 1975.
BP (Sp)	'Bahá'í Prayers for Special Occasions' section of *Bahá'í Prayers.*
BRE	*Bahá'í References on Education.* Vol. I of *Bahá'í Teachers' Handbook.* Wilmette, Bahá'í Publishing Trust, 1970.
BWF	*Bahá'í World Faith.* A compilation. Wilmette, Bahá'í Publishing Trust, 1956.
CH	*The Chosen Highway.* Lady Blomfield. London, Wilmette: Bahá'í Publishing Trust, 1986.
DAL	*The Divine Art of Living.* A compilation. Mabel Hyde Paine. Wilmette, Bahá'í Publishing Trust, 1944.
DB	*The Dawn-Breakers, Nabíl's Narrative.* London, Bahá'í Publishing Trust, 1953. New York, Bahá'í Publishing Committee, 1932.
ESW	*Epistle to the Son of the Wolf.* Bahá'u'lláh. Wilmette, Bahá'í Publishing Committee, 1941.
FL	*Family Life.* Compiled by the Research Department of the Universal House of Justice, Haifa, Bahá'í World Centre, January 1982.

FWU	*Foundations of World Unity*. Compiled from talks given by 'Abdu'l-Bahá. Wilmette: Bahá'í Publishing Trust, 1979.
GFY	*Guidance for Youth*. London, Bahá'í Publishing Trust, 1969.
GL	*Gleanings from the Writings of Bahá'u'lláh*. London, Bahá'í Publishing Trust, 1949. Wilmette, Bahá'í Publishing Trust, 1951.
HDW	*The Heaven of Divine Wisdom*. Compiled by the Research Department of the Universal House of Justice. London: Bahá'í Publishing Trust, 1978. (Published in the US as *Consultation: A Compilation*, and in Australia as *Bahá'í Consultation: The Lamp of Guidance*.)
HW	*The Hidden Words*. Bahá'u'lláh. Wilmette, Bahá'í Publishing Trust, 1963.
KI	*Kitáb-i-Íqán. The Book of Certitude*. Bahá'u'lláh. London, Bahá'í Publishing Trust, 1961.
LG	*Lights of Guidance: A Bahá'í Reference File*. Helen Hornby (compiler). New Delhi, Bahá'í Publishing Trust, 1983.
LTB	*Let Thy Breeze Refresh Them*. London: Bahá'í Publishing Trust, 1976.
MB	*The Mission of Bahá'u'lláh*. George Townshend. Oxford, George Ronald, 1952.
MUHJ	*Messages from the Universal House of Justice, 1968–1973*. Wilmette, Bahá'í Publishing Trust, 1976.
PB	*The Proclamation of Bahá'u'lláh to the Kings and Leaders of the World*. Haifa: Bahá'í World Centre, 1967.
PBA	*Principles of Bahá'í Administration*. A compilation. London, Bahá'í Publishing Trust, 1950.
PBL	*The Pattern of Bahá'í Life*. Richard Backwell (compiler). London, Bahá'í Publishing Trust, 1983.
PP	*The Priceless Pearl*. Rúḥíyyih Rabbani. London, Bahá'í Publishing Trust, 1969.
PT	*Paris Talks*. 'Abdu'l-Bahá. London, Bahá'í Publishing Trust, 1951.
PTF	*Portals to Freedom*. Howard Colby Ives. Oxford, George Ronald, 1976.
PUP	*The Promulgation of Universal Peace*. 'Abdu'l-Bahá. Wilmette, Bahá'í Publishing Trust, 2nd edn 1982.

KEY TO REFERENCES

SAQ	*Some Answered Questions*. 'Abdu'l-Bahá. Collected and Translated from the Persian by Laura Clifford Barney. Wilmette, Bahá'í Publishing Trust, rev. edn 1981.
SC	*Synopsis and Codification of the Laws and Ordinances of the Kitáb-i-Aqdas*. The Most Holy Book of Bahá'u'lláh. The Universal House of Justice. Haifa, Bahá'í World Centre, 1973.
SDC	*The Secret of Divine Civilization*. 'Abdu'l-Bahá. Wilmette, Bahá'í Publishing Trust, 1957.
SLK	*Seeking the Light of the Kingdom*. Compiled by the Research Department of the Universal House of Justice. London: Bahá'í Publishing Trust, 1977. (Published in the US as *Bahá'í Meetings: The Nineteen Day Feast*.)
SMA	*The Spiritual Meaning of Adversity*. Mamie L. Seto. Wilmette, Bahá'í Publishing Committee, 1949.
SW	*Star of the West*. The Bahá'í Magazine, published from 1910 to 1933 from Chicago and Washington, DC, by official Bahá'í agencies. RP Oxford, George Ronald, 1978.
TA	*Tablets of 'Abdu'l-Bahá*. 'Abdu'l-Bahá. Vol. I, New York, Bahá'í Publishing Committee, 1909. Vol. II, Chicago, Bahá'í Publishing Society, 1915. Vol. III, New York, Bahá'í Publishing Committee, 1916.
TB	*Tablets of Bahá'u'lláh Revealed after the Kitáb-i-Aqdas*. Bahá'u'lláh. Haifa, Bahá'í World Centre, 1978.
W	*Women*. Compiled by the Research Department of the Universal House of Justice. London: Bahá'í Publishing Trust, 1986.
WTA	*Excerpts from the Will and Testament of 'Abdu'l-Bahá*. 'Abdu'l-Bahá. Manchester, Bahá'í Publishing Trust, 1950.

References

TO THE READER

1. GL p. 174 (UK) 175 (USA)
2. TA pp. 578–9 (BRE p. 7)

1. EDUCATION IN GENERAL

1. BNE p. 69
2. LTL p. 10
3. PP p. 161
4. LTL p. 30
5. PTF p. 63
6. BE p. 30
7. GL p. 198 (UK) 199 (USA)
8. TB p. 156
9. GL p. 5 (both)
10. GL p. 277 (UK) 278 (USA)
11. MUHJ 1968–73, p. 90
12. HWA No. 1
13. ADJ p. 21
14. PUP p. 190 (PBL pp. 47–8)
15. SAQ ch. 64 p. 235
16. SAQ ch. 64 pp. 236–7
17. BE p. 18
18. GL p. 8 (both)
19. BE p. 18
20. SAQ ch. 3, p. 8
21. BE p. 11
22. BE p. 3

23. ESW p. 27
24. ESW p. 26
25. ESW p. 19
26. SC p. 22
27. GL pp. 49–50 (both)

2. THE EDUCATION OF CHILDREN

1. BE p. 2
2. TB p. 128
3. TA p. 579 (DAL p. 63)
4. BE p. 8
5. SWA p. 142
6. TA pp. 579, 580 (DAL p. 63)
7. Deut. 5: 9 and Numbers 14: 18
8. BE p. 47
9. PT p. 162
10. BE pp. 48–9
11. BE pp. 51–2
12. BE p. 50
13. BE p. 52
14. BE p. 51
15. TB p. 128
16. FL p. 30
17. BE p. 6
18. Simone Weil, *Waiting on God* (Routledge and Kegan Paul, 1952, translated from the French by Emma Craufurd). The quotation is on p. 51, from the essay 'Reflections on the right use of school studies with a view to the love of God'.
19. BE p. 53
20. BE p. 7

3. CHARACTER TRAINING

1. BE p. 33
2. BE p. 55
3. SAQ ch. 57 p. 212
4. Ibid.
5. St. Matthew 25: 14–30
6. GL pp. 258–9 (UK) 259–60 (USA)
7. PUP p. 53
8. BE pp. 31–2
9. The Universal House of Justice, Convention Message 1976 (see *Bahá'í Journal*; No. 233, June 1976)

10. GL pp. 329–30 (UK) 330–31 (USA)
11. TA p. 415 (BRE p. 71)
12. TB p. 51
13. GL p. 77 (both)
14. TA p. 687 (BWF p. 367)
15. ESW p. 27
16. BE p. 4
17. BE p. 78
18. BE p. 75
19. TA p. 459 (BWF p. 384)
20. *Chambers' 20th Century Dictionary*
21. PB pp. 47–8
22. St. John 6: 60
23. GL p. 265 (UK) 266 (USA)
24. SWB pp. 77–8
25. GL p. 284 (UK) 285 (USA)
26. BE p. 24
27. TB p. 27
28. TB p. 68
29. HWA No. 2
30. St. Matthew 5: 38–44
31. WTA p. 15
32. SAQ ch. 77 pp. 270–71
33. PB p. 50
34. GL p. 341 (UK) 342 (USA)
35. DB p. 219 (UK) 303 (USA)
36. DB p. 54 (UK) 79–80 (USA)
37. BWF pp. 412–13
38. GL p. 253 (UK) 254 (USA)
39. SDC pp. 97–8
40. BE p. 75
41. Isaiah 1: 18
42. SC p. 24
43. GL p. 304 (UK) 305 (USA)
44. TB p. 88
45. KI p. 124
46. BE p. 4
47. BE p. 3
48. BE p. 36
49. BE p. 26
50. TA p. 69 (DAL p. 27)
51. GL p. 277 (UK) 278 (USA)
52. GL p. 105 (UK) 106 (USA)

53. BE p. 31
54. BE p. 46

4. FAMILY LIFE

1. BE p. 26
2. BE p. 42
3. SW Vol IX No. 7, p. 81 (BNE p. 144, rev. edn 1974)
4. TB p. 26
5. W p. 30
6. W p. 31
7. W p. 30
8. TA p. 606 (BE pp. 53–4)
9. BE p. 52
10. MUHJ p. 90
11. BE p. 53
12. BE p. 71
13. GPB p. 249
14. PUP p. 168 (BE p. 82)
15. TA pp. 262–3 (BE p. 54)
16. TA p. 342 (BE p. 54)
17. BE p. 46
18. SAQ ch. 57 p. 215
19. Ibid.
20. Ibid.
21. PUP pp. 180–81 (BE p. 83)
22. BE p. 81
23. FWU p. 76
24. PT p. 60
25. BE p. 24
26. BE pp. 24–5
27. BE pp. 70–71
28. BE p. 75
29. BE pp. 67–8
30. LTB p. 23 (not counting pictures)
31. HDW p. 11
32. HDW p. 8
33. HDW p. 7
34. Ibid.
35. PT p. 175
36. HDW p. 7
37. GL pp. 314–15 (UK) 315–16 (USA)
38. GL p. 330 (UK) 331 (USA)

39. GL pp. 331–2 (UK) 332–3 (USA)
40. St. John 17: 17
41. St. Augustine, *Tract on the Epistle of St. John*, vii. 8.
42. BP No. 30 p. 37
43. BP (Sp.) p. 10
44. ADJ p. 28
45. ADJ p. 64
46. GFY pp. 4–5
47. St. Matthew 18: 3
48. BWF p. 249
49. GL p. 259 (UK) 260 (USA)
50. BE p. 73
51. GL p. 128 (UK) 128–9 (USA)
52. ADJ p. 69
53. SMA pp. 20–21
54. BE p. 51
55. CH p. 98
56. TA p. 581 (BWF p. 334)
57. KI p. 65
58. H. Bonar (1808–89)

5. FIRST TEACH YOUR OWN SELF

1. GL p. 334 (UK) 335 (USA)
2. GL p. 276 (UK) 277 (USA)
3. Ibid.
4. TA p. 459 (PBL p. 41)
5. TA pp. 619–20 (BRE p. 39)
6. TA p. 202 (BRE pp. 55–6)
7. ADJ p. 30
8. GL p. 284 (UK) 285 (USA)
9. WTA p. 15
10. PTF p. 57 (1976)
11. St. Matthew 25: 14–30
12. PTF p. 55
13. KI pp. 123–4
14. KI p. 124
15. ADJ p. 25

6. FEASTS AND HOLY DAYS

1. MUHJ p. 90
2. SLK p. 8

3. LG p. 189
4. BA p. 21 (from the *Kitáb-i-Aqdas*)
5. PBA p. 39
6. GL p. 35 (both)
7. Ibid.
8. GPB pp. 153–5
9. The Universal House of Justice, Naw-Rúz Message 1974 (see *Bahá'í Journal*, No. 222, April 1974)
10. GL p. 7 (both)
11. SLK p. 10
12. SLK p. 8
13. BNE p. 90
14. CH p. 98
15. TA p. 581 (BWF p. 334)
16. SLK p. 10
17. Ibid.
18. TA p. 641 (BWF pp. 351–2)
19. PBA p. 57
20. GL p. 284 (UK) 285 (USA)
21. Acts of the Apostles 20: 35
22. GL p. 8 (both)
23. GL p. 315 (UK) 316 (USA)

7. TESTS

1. TA p. 324 (DAL p. 92)
2. GL p. 105 (UK) 106 (USA)
3. PT p. 110
4. Book of Job 13: 5
5. TB p. 51
6. TB p. 63
7. PP p. 161
8. BE p. 22
9. ESW p. 27
10. BE p. 23
11. SC p. 22
12. BE p. 45
13. BP (Sp) p. 48
14. St. John 8: 31–2
15. GL pp. 334 (UK) 335–6 (USA)
16. Ibid.
17. PTF p. 63
18. PT p. 178

19. SMA pp. 17–18
20. TA pp. 579–80 (DAL p. 63)
21. Qur'án 29: 1
22. St. Mark 9: 24
23. St. Matthew 22: 14
24. TA p. 262 (BRE p. 6)
25. BE pp. 30–31

APPENDIX

1. FL pp. 30–33

EPILOGUE

1. MB pp. 147–8